BLESSED BE THE LORD

96

Albert McNally

Blessed be the Lord

PRAYING WITH ST LUKE

the columba press

First published in 2009 by
the columba press
55A Spruce Avenue, Stillorgan Industrial Park,
Blackrock, Co Dublin

Cover by Bill Bolger
Origination by The Columba Press
Printed in Ireland by ColourBooks Ltd, Dublin

ISBN 978-1-85607-651-7

Nihil Obstat
Paul Fleming
Censor Deputatus

Imprimatur
+ Patrick Walsh
Bishop of Down and Connor
25 January 2008

Contents

FOREWORD

'Lord, teach us to pray.'

Countless times these words of the followers of Jesus have risen from the lips, the hearts, of those who realise the importance of prayer in their lives but who struggle to pray. Where can we learn about prayer? We must begin with the Word of God in sacred scripture. In the Psalms in the Old Testament we have that wonderful corpus of prayer, of petition, of sorrow, of thanksgiving, of praise of God; but it is above all in the New Testament, in the gospels, that we learn from the teaching of Christ and from the many examples of his own life of prayer.

We can learn about prayer and yet not pray. We all find prayer difficult because we find it hard to focus our thoughts, to concentrate our minds – and so a prayer book can be a great help to us, provided we do not use a prayer book simply to say prayers, rather than to pray.

Fr McNally has placed in our hands a prayer book, Praying with St Luke, the gospel which is rightly called 'The gospel of prayer'. He offers reflections on 21 passages from St Luke's gospel, unlocking the gospel text, so that it becomes for us a source of prayer, a personal prayer book. Each passage is unlocked by four words – journey, joy, personal, challenge.

These reflections will be helpful to individual people; they will be especially helpful to leaders of parish prayer groups following the time-honoured method of prayer known as *Lectio Divina*, Divine Reading, and it is a grace of our time that prayer groups are becoming more and more a feature of the life or many parishes.

I warmly commend this prayer book and I thank Fr McNally for sharing with us his knowledge, his love and his own praying of St Luke's gospel. May all who use it be drawn into a deeper life of prayer, into that atmosphere of prayer in which Our Lord himself lived his life on earth.

+ Patrick Walsh,
Bishop of Down and Connor, 28th January 2008

PREFACE

This project was conceived just after the Millennium, when a group of priests in Down and Connor diocese dreamed of offering to parishes and prayer groups a simple guide to praying with St Luke's gospel. Due to practical difficulties the dream remained a dream, and it is only after many years of stolen intervals from a busy pastor's timetable that I am able to offer what is intended to be a user-friendly tool to those who are learning to pray with the scriptures. That it is not as simple as first planned reflects the years of growth.

My thanks to those members of diocesan prayer groups and a few friends who read parts of the text in draft and gave me useful advice and encouragement. My thanks also to the people of the parish of Maghera (Newcastle and Bryansford) who have allowed me to try out some of the gospel passages with them and given me feedback, which inspired me to keep going. My thoughts are with the Prayer Guides of Down and Connor and Dromore dioceses, with leaders of parish prayer groups who are doing such good work, but often lack the necessary background knowledge to give them confidence, with the clergy whose busy schedule does not allow much time for preparation though they wish to respond to their people's desire to pray with the scriptures, and with the many individuals who are trying on their own to nourish their prayer life using the gospels. My aim is to help them to pray, and to help them in their great work of leading others in prayer with the gospel of Luke, as perhaps the most congenial gospel to use as an introduction to sustained prayer with the word of God.

Perseverance in prayer is never easy. I have plenty of personal experience of beginning with enthusiasm and rapidly falling away. But to pray with Luke is not beyond most of us and, with a little effort, becomes increasingly life-giving.

As a busy pastor, I have not been able to keep up with all that is being written about St Luke. I gladly acknowledge a long standing debt to the work of Professor Albert Vanhoye, formerly of the Biblical Institute in Rome, who opened our eyes to the distinctive characteristics of the synoptic gospels, Matthew, Mark and Luke, in the late sixties. Much has been written since then, but his work gave me the impetus to attempt to translate the insights of those who write commentaries into something accessible, at parish level, to groups or individuals who are seeking to be nurtured by the word of God. With the help of the Holy Spirit, if we listen to Jesus speaking to us, perhaps we may be able to say with the disciples on the road to Emmaus, 'Were not our hearts burning within us while he talked to us on the road, while he was opening the scriptures to us?' (Luke 24:32).

Albert McNally
Parish of Maghera
January 2009

INTRODUCTION

My purpose is to help readers to imitate Luke's wonderful models of prayer, Mary the model disciple who glorifies the Lord in the *Magnificat*, and Zechariah who blesses the Lord in the *Benedictus*. Praying with St Luke's gospel will increase our awareness of how richly blessed we are through God's word and his presentation of Jesus, so that we will be prompted to respond with joyful praise, wonder and delight, to bless and glorify the Lord. 'Blessed be the Lord God of Israel, for he has looked favourably on his people and redeemed them.' (*The Benedictus*, 1:68)

St Luke's is a very prayerful gospel. Jesus gives the example of prayer, being seen at prayer more often in Luke that in the other gospels. As is known, Luke shows Jesus at prayer before any major decision or turning point on his journey (baptism, choosing the Twelve, the agony etc.). He tells his disciples how to pray (read, e.g. 11:1-13). So you may be tempted to open at Session 1 and begin right away, but it is advisable to read this introduction first, at least the section headed *Suggested Approach to Luke*. And if you are setting out to lead a group, you will need to become familiar with the procedures set out here.

Our starting point is this: each evangelist has his own insight into the mystery of our salvation through Jesus, so we will seek to learn from and respond to Luke's particular way of understanding Jesus. Of course he shares much in common with Mark and Matthew and at times John, but the differences are clues to his point of view, as are the things he adds and the things he leaves out. The more we understand that, the better we will be able to pray with Luke.

A methodology and some tools are necessary. As tools I offer four *key words* that are easy to remember and applicable to almost any passage in the gospel. As methodology I offer a brief description of the ancient method of prayer called 'divine reading' (*lectio divina*), adapted for our use. You may of course pray with Luke using a short text, even individual verses, but doing so tends to isolate each text from its context, and I prefer to work with longer passages where we may more easily see the writer's intention. Each passage offered here is meant to give food for thought for at least a week (after which it is suggested that then you may select a short text to carry in your mind and heart). I have tended to err on the side of giving abundance of material, at the risk of demonstrating the poverty of my own prayer life! Readers are urged to use their discretion, and swallow only what they are able to digest for their personal prayer, and if their own thoughts soar far beyond my own, no one will be happier than myself. Remember: there is no necessity to use all the material given at any one time, or to use more than one or two of the four suggested keys to open up a given text.

SUGGESTED APPROACH TO ST LUKE

First tool: The Motif of Journeying

Luke likes the motif of journeying, often a physical journey, but really a faith journey, or a pilgrimage, a journey that seeks truth and enlightenment, in the company of the best of leaders, along with others who seek to find God. We are disciples of Jesus, following him on a *journey of faith*. He has journeyed before us, a journey which Luke describes as an 'exodus' (9:31), and our reading of the gospel can be seen as our prayerful accompaniment of Jesus on that most important journey from Galilee to Jerusalem, to his death and resurrection and through death to the Father. The Risen Jesus also accompanies us on our journey, for disciples must follow him on that exodus to the Father. His walking with the disciples on the road to Emmaus (24:13-35) shows that he walks with disciples always, even when they do not recognise him. At the end of the gospel, Jesus commissions disciples to carry his word on the great journey to all nations, beginning from Jerusalem. The motif of *Journey* will be our first key to praying with St Luke.

We are called to journey with Jesus in three ways: (i) to walk with him as a disciple (that is, a 'learner') through the gospel journey, to accompany him, with the aid of Luke's insights, as he travels the roads of the Holy Land to his 'passover' (*exodus*) in Jerusalem; (ii) to allow him to walk the journey of our lives with us, that we may listen to him, know ourselves to be disciples, and be witnesses to him; (iii) to allow him to lead us on our inner

11

journey, so that we may come to know and love him, and in so doing to come to know and love ourselves, as people who are richly blessed in him.

Second tool: Personal Relationship

Luke's introduction helps us to find the second key. He tells us he writes to help a man called Theophilus. 'I have decided to write an orderly account for you, most excellent Theophilus, so that you may know the truth concerning the things about which you have been instructed' (1:3-4). Theophilus may well have been a historical person, but he equally stands for every disciple who reads the gospel of Luke:

– Theophilus means 'lover of God';
– he has already some knowledge of the story of Jesus;
– he needs to know it better.

That is you, and I, and any of us!

This makes Luke's gospel ideal to read and study on one's own, knowing it is addressed to a 'you', a believer in Jesus who would like to know more. So when I read it I may see it as a message addressed to me personally, which can help me to grow in the knowledge and love of Jesus, and of the Father, so that I may become really a Theophilus (or a Theophila), a lover of God. This may be chrystalised for memory purposes in the word *Personal*. By personal I mean that it is about my personal relationship with Jesus, and through him, my relationship to God and to all Jesus' brothers and sisters. We will find that Luke loves to stress the close personal relationship of Jesus with his Father, a relationship cultivated in deep prayer. He stresses also that Jesus carries out his mission filled with the Holy Spirit, and how Jesus relates in love and compassion to each individual he meets on his journey. So I can read this gospel to come to know Jesus' love for me, and through that relationship I will be brought into close relationship with the Father, with the Holy Spirit, and with the community of believers. It is not that Luke is proposing an individualistic religion, just my private relationship with God. But he knows that all community begins with the conviction that we are personally loved, and then we are able to join the community of disciples who are his witnesses to the world.

Third tool: A Joyful Message

Disciples in Luke, beginning with Mary, Zechariah and Simeon, sing out their joy and thanksgiving for the blessings of salvation brought by Jesus. Their songs became the joyful response of the Christian community for the blessings of salvation and the gift of the Holy Spirit. The reader is invited to join in the great act of joyful thanksgiving, even in the midst of the sorrows of life. So a very important key is *Joy*, reminding us to look for the good news in each passage, and to give praise to God for his goodness.

Fourth tool: A Challenging Message

Luke challenges me, as he challenges Theophilus, to listen to the story of Jesus, to get to know him better and learn to act like him. Luke's gospel does emphasise the love and compassion of Jesus for the poor, the outcast, the marginalised. Matthew's 'Be perfect as your heavenly Father is perfect' (5:48), becomes in Luke, 'Be compassionate, just as your Father is compassionate' (6:36, NRSV 'merciful'). But do not be complacent! Because Luke has great personal loyalty to Jesus, he believes that Jesus demands from his disciples the same undivided loyalty. There is no such thing as half discipleship in Luke. 'If any want to become my followers, let them deny themselves and take up their cross daily and follow me' (9:23) – Luke is the only evangelist to add 'daily'! Our fourth key is *Challenge*. In every Lucan passage there will be an explicit or implicit challenge to the reader to follow the example of Jesus or of his disciples. We will look for the challenge and try to respond to it.

Key Words

The proposed method is simple. Approach each section with four keys, which will help you to unlock the text in a prayerful way. These keys are not meant to be exhaustive – there are many other possible approaches. These four are to help you on the way, something to fall back on when your own thoughts are sluggish. They do overlap, of course, and that need not worry us. That they overlap is in fact useful to those who wish to use only one of the key words at a time, and come back to the text to use another one later. They are simply different ways of trying to reflect on the richness of a text, different search words scanning the text, like different aspects of the same person. In group work or in private prayer, you do not need to use all four every time (sometimes one or other is less easy to apply). In group work, the leader should decide how many of them can be used in the time available, and allow the members of the group to continue the prayer on their own with the other keys. For private prayer, a different key may be used on succeeding days, with each passage taking a week or more to digest thoroughly. And if your own prayer takes wing without any of them, so much the better.

The four suggested key words: *Journey, Joy, Personal, Challenge.*

LECTIO DIVINA (DIVINE READING)

This time-honoured method of praying with the scriptures is becoming familiar again to more and more people. It profitably combines learning and praying about the text, and so avoids the twin dangers of an academic study that fails to warm the heart, or the reading of our own preconceptions into the text without asking what the sacred author was trying to say and what the church tells us through her biblical scholars. The method has four main stages, described briefly below, though it is always wise to begin by *focusing* our attention with silence, a candle or icon, some music where appropriate, and certainly a fervent prayer for divine help as we explore the word.

Lectio (reading): that is, reading until you are familiar with the text, and have thought about its meaning, studied if you have to. We are going to call it *Familiarisation.* The basic minimum is always attentive reading (and re-reading) of the text, with great respect for it as the word of God speaking to us. Studying the *background* to the text is really part of 'reading'. For each passage selected, I give the text, and then background information. Our temptation is to jump into the next stage before we have really digested the text, and to omit the sometimes dry as dust background. But you will profit from reading the text, perhaps noting what you find difficult or puzzling, what seem to be the key ideas, and then reading the background, before returning to the text with clearer vision. For the early monks, 'reading' meant reading until they knew the text by heart. So do not rush it, especially, strangely enough, with a text that is very well known to you. Over familiarity often means that we do not really listen to the text as we should.

Meditatio (meditation): thinking about the passage, its meaning in the time of Jesus, its meaning for me now. This is where the key words come in: they are tools to help us to reflect on the text. We will call this stage *Reflection*. Remember that it is all right to concentrate on some ideas in the text, so long as we do not isolate them from the context in which Luke has put them, and to use one or two of the key words at any particular time. At this stage we deepen our understanding of the text, and try to grasp the feelings and responses of the people in the narrative. Some people find it easy enough to see themselves in the story, and to react as if they were there when it all happened, and are able to feel the emotions of the bystanders and hear and speak to Jesus or the disciples. Others find this more difficult, and need to bring the story as it were into the present time, by thinking of similar experiences or situations in their own lives, and asking what Jesus has to say to them now, in their own daily struggle to keep close to him.

Oratio (Prayer): a prayerful response to what we see as the message of the passage. This can take the form of spontaneous prayer, or may be structured into acts of adoration, contrition, thanksgiving, and petition (supplication) – the word 'acts' is a memory aid. So for example, the key 'joy' prompts us to give joyful praise of God for his goodness to us in Christ, the key 'challenge' calls for decisions about our future in the light of the word of God we have been hearing. We will use the word *Response* for this stage. Though I will always make suggestions for response, it is very important that these should be fall-back suggestions, to be used if necessary, after and not instead of your own personal response. Remember also that even if you only use one of the key words for reflection, you should always try to make a response in prayer before ending your prayer time. Leaders of groups should always allow a period of quiet to facilitate individual response.

Contemplatio (contemplation): for our purposes this means allowing the sacred text to become part of our conscious and subconscious minds, allowing the word of God to resonate in us. The Holy Spirit is able to work in us, allowing us insights and keeping us close to the Lord in ways we cannot predict. We will be suggesting the choice of a short text from each passage to keep turning over in our minds. We keep for our fourth stage the word *Contemplation*. It becomes an awareness that we are disciples of the living Lord who is always with us.

We will use this *Lectio Divina* method with some care firstly with the *Magnificat* as an example for those who are not very familiar with it. After that keep before you the stages:
> *Focus, Familiarisation, Reflection, Response, Contemplation,*
> and our four Key Words,
> *Journey, Joy, Personal and Challenge* (used at the *Reflection* stage).

The Magisterium Encourages us to use Lectio Divina
The *Instrumentum Laboris* (Vatican City 2008), the agenda document for the October 2008 Synod of Bishops on 'The Word of God in the Life and Mission of the Church', gives great encouragement to those who are using *Lectio Divina*. 'Praying with the Word of God is a privileged experience, traditionally called *Lectio Divina* ... The whole church seems again to be giving specific attention to *Lectio Divina* ... Some see the need to take into consideration the real possibilities among the faithful and adapt this classic form to different situations in such a way as to conserve the essence of this reading in prayer, while highlighting its nutritive value for a person's faith ... Today, however, the Spirit, through the Magisterium, proposes *Lectio Divina* as an effective pastoral instrument and a valuable tool in the church in the education and formation of priests, in the everyday lives of consecrated women and men, in parish communities, in families, associations and movements and in the ordinary believer – both young and old – who can find in this form of reading a practical, accessible means ... to come into contact with the Word of God.' (#38)

Vatican II, *Constitution on Divine Revelation*, #21: 'Remember that prayer should accompany the reading of sacred scripture, so that God and his people may talk together; for "we speak to him when we pray; we hear him when we read the divine sayings"...'

ADVICE FOR USE

These sessions are to be used in a flexible way, and are suitable for either private or group use. There is nothing particularly important about the sequence of passages chosen, though the reflection on the *Magnificat* should always be used as a starter, unless participants are already familiar with the process. Neither is there anything particularly significant about the number of selections treated, three groups of seven passages. The number seven has good biblical vibrations, but there is no need to work through all the passages, or even a set of seven, at one time, and my hope is that the method will encourage users to attempt to pray with other passages from St Luke.

Lent and Advent are good times to begin. Some of these reflections began as Lent and Advent sessions in the parish of Maghera, in Down and Connor diocese. For the four Sundays of Advent, the sequence Magnificat, Annunciation, Nativity, Baptism may be used. In Lent the passion-resurrection selections are appropriate: six sessions may be chosen from the final seven. For the purpose of introducing people to guided prayer and *lectio divina*, a group leader may make a personal choice, and encourage participants to try others on their own. For a private retreat, especially for people who are increasingly chronologically challenged like myself, I suggest (1) the Magnificat, (6) Call and Response, (9) the Transfiguration, (15) the Last Supper, (18) the Crucifixion, and either (20) Emmaus or (21) Jesus Commissions Witnesses.

Preparations
The leader should arrange for some helpers to set up the room, with chairs in a semicircle (or semicircles depending on numbers). Provision should be made for music, and a table arranged in the centre with an open Bible, a candle, and perhaps a crucifix, an icon or picture of the Madonna and Child. Decisions need to have been made about possible refreshments afterwards, and preparations made.

Welcome
The leader should welcome everyone to the meeting, provide music and a lighted candle. The leader should announce the chosen text for the session, and make sure that everyone has access to a copy.

1. Focus
Encourage the group to settle down, sit comfortably but upright in their chairs. Ask them to focus their minds on their bodies, feel the chair, become aware of their bodily tensions, gradually relax shoulders and muscles, breathe deeply, become aware of their breathing. Invoke the Holy Spirit, the breath of God, who breathes life into us, and who has breathed life into (inspired) the word of God; ask the Spirit to breathe into each person in the room, to come with his gifts of understanding and warmth and guide our thoughts as we prepare to hear the word of God.

Allow a few moments silence, then say the opening prayer, either together or through a chosen volunteer.

2. Familiarisation
Attentive reading: The chosen text may be read aloud, slowly and clearly, and the members encouraged to read it again quietly. Allow time for them to become familiar with the 'shape' of the text (leaders may give prompts), the narrative sequence, and leading ideas, the actions and/or words of Jesus, and the reactions of his listeners. People may be encouraged to close their eyes and try to retell the story as clearly as they can to themselves – and then check the text again. It is helpful if they note difficulties which may be clarified in Background Notes.

2.1 Background: background notes are given for each passage. Part of the 'reading' of a text is to clarify difficulties, to understand the context of the passage and the particular way the author has treated the passage. When the background material has been read, it is important to re-read the passage in the light of what has been discovered. Leaders may attempt to answer questions and clarify misunderstandings, but should not allow it to become too time consuming.

Note: In the initial session, all this will have to be done in the group. The leader may decide to highlight the important points for the group. In the following sessions, members should be encouraged to read the text and study the background notes in advance. This will enable the group to move on to the *Reflection* stage more quickly. The leader may judge that another period of silence is necessary before moving into the *Reflection* stage.

3. Reflection

To help the group members to reflect on the passage, one or more of the Key Words may be chosen, *Journey, Joy, Personal, Challenge*, to help to open up the passage for them. In an initial session, the leader may have to guide the group, with prompts and questions. Encourage a mixture of group discussion and silence for thought. When the group becomes more familiar with the process, encourage them to do their own reflection on the Key Words, either as a whole group, or in small groups, or individually, before consulting the material offered in the notes. Prompt questions are: How do the events/words in this passage affect Jesus or his companions? What do they tell us about Jesus? His disciples? His opponents? Can you identify with the disciples, or indeed with his opponents? What are their feelings, decisions, attitudes, misunderstandings? Do you experience those same feelings and attitudes in your lives? How is Jesus challenging our attitudes here? What do you find hopeful and joyful about this passage? What do you find difficult, challenging?

4. Response

How does our reflection move us to pray in response? Use our feelings of gratitude, joy, repentance, our desire to change, to be closer to Jesus, as guides for our thoughts and prayers. Some may simply need to be silent in the presence of the Lord, aware of his love and goodness. Others may need to put words on their thoughts and feelings. What are we challenged to do in response to this passage? How do we need to change? Use the suggestions in the notes only after you have tried to make your own response. It is vital that the leader watches the time and allows adequate space for this part of the prayer.

5. Contemplation

The leader should encourage the members not to allow the prayer to end when they leave the session, but to let the feelings, attitudes remain with them as they return to their normal routines. Ask them to choose a short text from the passage that they will be able to turn over in their minds, to remind them of what they experienced during the prayer session. Encourage them to use the other Key Words for which there may not have been time in the group session, and to respond to them in their own way. Then the closing prayer may be said.

Preparation for the next session: announce the time, place, date of the next session, and the text that will be used. Emphasise the importance of reading the text and the background material beforehand.

Group Leaders

The sessions are intended to be fairly self-explanatory, and no great professional expertise is required – just some experience of attempting to pray with the scriptures, time to prepare, some courage, and some organisational skill (delegation helps here!). Some of these sessions have been tried and tested with parish groups and they do work. The group leader needs to be patient, set the scene or delegate the setting of the scene, help the group to focus. Encourage people to share reflections but do not force them. Do not be alarmed that there will usually be more than the group can cope with in a session – this material is meant to be lived with, and the reflection to be continued. With beginners the leader may decide to allow them to read the reflection section on a particular Key Word before some discussion of it and sharing of insights; but once familiar with the process, members should be encouraged to try to apply the Key Word to the text themselves, individually or in small groups. Allow quiet time for personal response in prayer. Do not be afraid to say, 'enough for now', and recommend continued reflection on their own.

Before beginning, group leaders need to be familiar with the background material offered for each session. A few helpful commentaries are listed below, but group leaders do not need to know everything. It is not necessary to solve all difficulties in order to be prayerful. We will always find enough food for our prayer in the parts we can handle, content to stand in wonder before the mysteries. It is helpful for the leader, time permitting, to have tried to pray with the passage beforehand, and to be prepared to offer examples of how to apply the Key Words, in order to get things rolling. Be aware of the leader's temptation: to facilitate others to pray, and neglect to do it personally. The group will carry you along. Do not be afraid! The group leader has to arrange for the set up, ensure some silence (don't be afraid to let it last), to decide when it is time to move on to the next stage, to try to ensure that no participant dominates with too much talk, to be sensitive to those who wish to remain silent, or gently encourage them, and to end it. In work with groups I have tried to fit everything into an hour, with time for a little look back at the previous session, and time to indicate the text for the next session so that people may prepare in advance. Some prayers are offered for beginning and end, but your own prayers or those of a group member will be better.

A simplified schema for each session is given at the end of the end of this introduction. This may be photocopied and enlarged if necessary.

Beginners
Attempting to pray with a passage of scripture for the first time is a new experience, different from 'saying prayers'. People sometimes try to be more prayerful by saying more prayers, and it does not always work. If we feel dissatisfied with our prayer life, or are tormented by 'distractions', God may in fact be calling us to pray in a new way. Often our 'saying prayers' is a one-way street, ourselves talking, with no opportunity for God to get a word in edgeways! People tell me that God is not listening to

them, when I suspect it is the other way round. The normal way for God to speak to us, to tell us about his love for us, and what he would like us to do, is through his word in the scriptures. So we have to steel ourselves to be quiet and to practise 'active listening'. This means paying careful attention to the words of scripture, seeing them as addressed to us, asking the Holy Spirit to help us to understand, and trying to respond in words that come from our own hearts, allowing our insights and our feelings to guide our response in prayer. For most of us, words are necessary. For some, words are unnecessary; they are able just to be present to the Lord in peace and trust.

Sorry to say, the word of God, though powerful, does not work by magic! Our minds and feelings have to be engaged, with the help of the Holy Spirit. To take a simple example, if someone asks you to do something for them, nothing will happen if you do not *hear* the request, or do not *understand* it (if it comes from someone who does not speak your language), or do not realise that the request *is addressed to you*, or have no intention of doing anything for this particular person. Even the Holy Spirit has trouble working on us through the word, unless we *hear it* (pay attention to it), *understand it* (sometimes we need to ask questions, do some research or study), see it *as addressed to us*, and be prepared *to act upon it*. So it requires *attention, understanding, involvement, openness*. If you add *excitement* to cover the feelings of warmth, gratitude, love, wonder and delight that the Holy Spirit may cause to rise up in you as you rediscover God's tender mercy towards you in Jesus Christ, then the initial vowels may help you to remember them, even if not in the usual order (a u i o e)!

The Holy Spirit, who was at work in the writing of the scriptures (we call that 'inspiration'), is also at work when the faithful listen attentively with openness to the word of God speaking to us now. Sometimes we find re-cognition (a re-knowing) of something we have always deep down known, and therefore an affirming experience, which will become a source of strength and nourishment for our spiritual lives. We begin by trusting that Jesus is really present in his word, as he is really present in the Eucharist; we can talk to him in both presences, and be nourished by him. 'One does not live by bread alone, but by every word that comes from the mouth of God' (Deuteronomy 8:3, quoted by Jesus when tempted in the desert). Then we can acquire the habit of holding short texts of scripture in our minds and hearts, so that we can go on praying about them while we work or go about our daily routines. Jesus' words, 'I am with you always' (Matthew 28:20) can take on a new meaning for us. I invite you to give it a try, and God be with you! 'The Lord make his face to shine upon you, and be gracious to you' (Numbers 6:25).

Translations of the Bible

In the text, I have used the *New Revised Standard Version* (NRSV). I find it helpful to provide a 'structured' text, partly because it is a very useful exercise for getting the feel and shape of a passage, partly because I find it helpful if everyone in a group uses the same version. But it is not essential. Many people have a favourite translation, and using one's own Bible allows easy reference to other texts.

The NRSV is a comparatively recent version of the *Revised Standard Version* (RSV), and has the benefits of remaining fairly close to the original text, and using inclusive language. The RSV is also usable. *The Jerusalem Bible* (JB), now available as the *New Jerusalem Bible,* is readable, with section headings and notes, but being a translation from the French, is a little bit further from the original text. The Catholic *New American Bible* (NAB) is an up to date translation in more contemporary language. The *New English Bible* (NEB) represents modern British Protestant scholarship. The *New International Version* (NIV) is produced by international Evangelical scholars. The *Good News Bible* is a more popular and down to earth translation, easier for a beginner to handle, but not so close to the original text. If you wish to be jogged out of over familiarity with the text, try *The New Testament*, translated by Nicholas King SJ (Kevin Mayhew, 2004).

SELECT BIBLIOGRAPHY

Joseph A Fitzmeyer, *The Gospel According to Luke*, 2 Vols, Anchor Bible Series, Doubleday , 1981. (The most complete commentary by a well known American Catholic scholar, but a little daunting).

Luke Timothy Johnston, *The Gospel of Luke*, Sacra Pagina Series, Michael Glazier/Liturgical Press 1991. Strong (perhaps too focused) on Jesus as Prophet.

Dennis McBride CSsR, *The Gospel of Luke, A Reflective Commentary*, Costello Publishing Company, New York, 1982.

Craig A Evans, *Luke, New International Biblical Commentary* (based on NIV), Paternoster Press, 1995.

William Kunz SJ, *Following Jesus, A Disciple's Guide to Luke and Acts*, Servant Books, Ann Arbor, Michigan, 1984.

Eugene La Verdiere, *Luke*, Veritas 1980.

Carlo Cardinal Martini, *Praying with St Luke*, Veritas 1987.

Michel de Verteuil, *Lectio Divina with the Sunday Gospels, the Year of Luke, Year C*, The Columba Press, 2004.

M Basil Pennington, *Lectio Divina, Renewing the Ancient Practice of Praying the Scriptures*, Crossroad Publishing Company, New York, 1998.

Jean Khoury, *Lectio Divina, Spiritual Reading of the Bible*, CTS, London 2006.

Thelma Hall, *Too Deep for Words, Rediscovering Lectio Divina*, Paulist Press, New York/ Mahwah 1988.

Stephen J. Binz, *Conversing with God in Scripture*, The Word Among Us Press, Maryland, USA, 2008.

GROUP MEETINGS

* Welcome

1. FOCUS
    Opening Prayer

2. FAMILIARISATION
    Attentive Reading of the text
    2.1 Studying the Background

3. REFLECTION
    3.1 Journey
    3.2 Joy
    3.3 Personal
    3.4 Challenge

4. RESPONSE

5. CONTEMPLATION

Closing Prayer

SECTION A: PREPARING FOR THE JOURNEY

Session 1: The Magnificat (Luke 1:46-55)

1. FOCUS

Focus the mind and heart on God's presence. In groups, the leader should welcome everyone, play some soothing music, encourage them to sit comfortably, relax shoulders and muscles. Breathe slowly and evenly from the diaphragm. Use a candle, icon, picture of the Madonna and Child, or whatever helps to still the mind. Ask the Holy Spirit to help you to listen to the word of God and understand it better.

Prayer: God our Father, Mary is the model disciple, who gave thanks and praise to you in her *Magnificat* for the blessings she received. Help us to learn from her prayer how to be grateful for the blessings we have received through Christ her son, and how to magnify your name. Pour out your Spirit into our hearts, that the Spirit may guide us in our listening to your word, and in our prayer of thanksgiving. We ask this through Christ our Lord. Amen.

2. FAMILIARISATION

Note: Familiarisation includes reading the text carefully, reading the background notes (2.1 below), and then rereading the text.

Read the Magnificat slowly (a few times), preferably aloud. Take time to really look at it. Sometimes we are so familiar with a text or prayer that we do not really hear the words! Notice how it is set out (explained below). Note how Mary begins with joyful praise (introduction), then lists at least four reasons ('because', 'for') for her thanksgiving; then she praises God's qualities – the strength of his arm, his love for the poor and the hungry, his reversal of roles between the poor and the rich. The conclusion sums up: This is one more, and the greatest, example of God's fidelity to his promises since the time of Abraham.

Introduction

46   And Mary said
       My soul magnifies the Lord,

47   and my spirit rejoices in God my Saviour;

Body

48   for [because] he has looked with favour on the lowliness
       of his servant.
       Surely [=for, because] from now on all generations will
       call me blessed;

49   for the Mighty One has done great things for me,
       and holy is his name.

50   [Because] His mercy is for those who fear him
       from generation to generation.

51   He has shown strength with his arm;
       he has scattered the proud in the thoughts of their hearts.

52   He has brought down the powerful from their thrones,
       and lifted up the lowly;

53   he has filled the hungry with good things,
       and sent the rich away empty.

Conclusion

54   He has helped his servant Israel,
       in remembrance of his mercy,

55   according to the promise he made to our ancestors,
       to Abraham and to his descendants for ever.

2.1 Background

Background material will be offered for each session. Recommended procedure is to read the text first, note things that you would like to know more about, pick out things that strike you as important. Then read this background material before attempting to pray with the passage, or before a group session. It is important for group leaders especially to be familiar with it beforehand. Read the text again in the light of this background, before you move on to the Reflection stage.

    2.1.1 Something technical to begin: In structure the *Magnificat* resembles a Psalm of Praise (e.g. 1 Samuel 2:1-10 – on which it is loosely based; Psalms 8, 9, 29, 33, 100, 117 etc.). These psalms commonly have three parts:

- An *introduction* praising God.
- The *body* of the psalm lists the motives for praise, usually beginning with a 'because' clause. Motives include God's deeds for individuals or for his people, and God's qualities – power, wisdom, mercy etc.
- A *conclusion*, fairly flexible, which may retell the motives, include a blessing or request, or generalise – God is always like this.

Therefore the text of Mary's prayer has been set out in three sections above. Have another look at it, identify the three parts, and see the reasons Mary gives for praising the Lord. The conclusion is, God has always been faithful to his promises to Abraham and his descendants, and this promise of a Son to Mary who will restore the line of David is the newest and most wonderful proof of God's fidelity and love.

2.1.2 The Poor of the Lord: For Luke, the Magnificat sums up the spirituality of Mary and of those who appear in these early chapters of the gospel – Zechariah, Elizabeth, Simeon and Anna in the temple. Their spirituality represents the best of the late Israelite tradition, those who are called 'the Poor of the Lord' (*anawim*), people who realise that after the fall of Jerusalem and the House of David, though poor in every other way, they are rich because they hope in God who is faithful to his promises. Therefore they trust that God will send a Messiah to restore the line of David, look forward to it expectantly, and rejoice when it happens. This joy bursts out in canticles of *praise* from Mary, Elizabeth, Zechariah, and Simeon, results in *contemplation* (pondering in the heart, 1:66, 2:19), and glad *sharing of the good news* with others (Mary and Elizabeth, 1:39ff, the shepherds 2:17, Anna 2:38). Through our praying with St Luke, let the Spirit lead us to those three things: praise, contemplation, and sharing the good news.

2.1.3 Early Christian Canticles of Praise: The spirituality of these canticles represents also the joyful response of the early Christians to the wonderful blessings they have received through the birth, ministry, death and resurrection of Jesus. The canticles are (at least) edited with that post-resurrection knowledge, so they are able to be Christian prayers praising God for all the blessings received through the Risen Lord. The church has always prayed them as such, e.g., in the daily *Prayer of the Church*. This allows each of us to make them our own, in thanksgiving for the personal blessings we have received through Jesus. Placed at the beginning of the gospel, they give a tone to the whole gospel, and suggest an approach that will help us greatly in our personal prayers. Try to read the text again as your prayer, thanking God for sending us his Beloved Son, and for having called you to be his disciple.

2.1.4 The context of Mary's prayer is her visit to her cousin Elizabeth (1:39-56). Her meeting with Elizabeth, happily pregnant with John the Baptist, is an emotional and Spirit-filled occasion, when the two burst out in thankful praise to God, first Elizabeth, 'Blessed are you among women, and blessed is the fruit of your womb' (1:42), then Mary, 'My soul magnifies the Lord ...' The Holy Spirit uses people to inspire each other. So if you are in a prayer group for the first time, take courage.

3. REFLECTION
In a group session, unless the familiarisation has been done beforehand (unlikely in a first meeting), it may be necessary to focus again, as above.

We now begin to reflect prayerfully on the Magnificat. Approach with courage, like the 'Poor of the Lord', putting your trust not in yourself but in God. This is where we allow God to speak to us through the text. We are going to use the Key Words, journey, joy, personal, challenge to help us. (Leaders decide whether the time permits the use of one or more of the key words, with the Response).

3.1 *Journey:* The canticle celebrates a new stage of the Israelite journey, the beginning of the era of the long-awaited Messiah. Mary has travelled from Nazareth to the hill country of Judea, which may be seen as symbolic of her personal journey. She does not yet fully comprehend where this journey will take her, but we know it will be a difficult road. We hope to follow that road as we read and reflect on other passages from Luke. It will be a journey following God's will, that his great plans may bear fruit, and she will travel willingly, trusting in God's fidelity. When Mary says 'Yes' to God's plan, she accepts the future in trust, wherever it will take her. As we set out on a prayer journey with St Luke, we may have fears about what God will ask of us, so we have to put our trust in God, like Mary. Do you feel ready to commit yourself to such a journey?

3.2 Joy: Read the text again with the word joy in mind; pick out words and phrases which indicate Mary's joy, and her sense of being mightily blessed. Mary feels humble, claiming no merits of her own, and is therefore so much the more filled with wonder and gratitude for God's choice of her to be the mother of the Messiah. She accumulates the reasons for her rejoicing: God has looked upon her with favour, all generations will call her blessed, the Mighty One has done great things for the lowly servant, and so on. She sees her call as one in a long line of God's favours to those who are humble. God gives hope to the poor by overturning the established order, choosing the poor instead of the rich and powerful. Her joy demands to be spoken. Mary has contained her joy until she visits Elizabeth, and when the two cousins get together there is a mutual outpouring of their emotions. Take a moment to be in mind and heart close to these two mothers-to-be in their thankfulness.

Since Mary's prayer has also become the prayer of the Christian community, we may now try to make it our own. We have many of the same reasons as Mary for being joyful, for the Lord has not just come among us, but has come to live in us. What great things has the Mighty God done for you through the coming of Jesus? Most of us, like Mary, stand in a line of people of faith who have handed on the gift of faith to us. Spend some time reflecting on the gifts you have received from God, from your parents, from the church. Do you feel that you could be more grateful for them? Would you be able to use them better if you appreciated them more? When you feel thankful, what are you prompted to say/do? Would you accept that a sense of being blessed by God is the basis of all our worship? Reflect that the word 'Eucharist' means thanksgiving, where we join with Jesus in thanking and praising God.

3.3 *Personal:* Mary has very personal reasons to give thanks to God, for herself as well as for her people. Now she is bound to God in a new and very close relationship. Read the text again, and note the uses of my, me, for me. But Mary as a Jewess would have been very conscious of being part of God's Covenant, the relationship of love that bound God and his people. Luke's personal presentation of the message is never about a private relationship with God: Mary sees her mission in terms of her people, and God's fidelity to her people ('to Abraham and his descendants for ever'). Note the qualities Mary attributes to herself: lowly, but to be seen as blessed for ever. Her blessings are not for herself alone, but for her people. This is the way God always acts, since the time of Abraham, always faithful to his people. Mary did not expect to be so blessed, but she rejoices in her blessings, and knows they will have to be used for the good of all the people.

Are you surprised, as Mary was, that the Lord should want to choose you as a disciple? You may feel that you are 'nobody special', and would not dare to say with Mary, 'My soul magnifies the Lord, my spirit rejoices in God my saviour ... for the Mighty one has done great things for me.' But though you may see yourself as 'nobody special', even if you feel unloved, that does not stop God from blessing you, as he blessed the lowliness of Mary, or from loving you. Humility does not allow us to compare ourselves with the mother of Jesus, of course. But humility is not about thinking we are nobodies, but about confessing that all our gifts come from God, not from ourselves, and knowing that God wants us to accept those gifts and use them. Like Mary, our blessings, e.g., baptism, confirmation, Eucharist, bring us into a very close personal relationship with God, one which we need to deepen through prayer. But it is never 'private'! Like Mary, we need to be conscious of being part of the community of faith, God's family, and be ready to use the gifts God has given us for the good of the whole family. Would you like to read the *Magnificat* again, at least in part, as your prayer?

3.4 *Challenge:* Mary is facing the tremendous challenge to carry out faithfully this divine commission to which she has just said 'Yes.' How does she face it? She has humility, but no holding back – God will give the strength to carry out her great mission. God brings down the powerful, lifts up the lowly, fills the hungry. As God helped Israel, so he will faithfully help Mary.

Our sense of being blessed is also a challenge for us. The challenge is to let that sense of being blessed influence our way of seeing and doing things, and to know that we have a personal mission to share the good news and build up the family of God. It is a challenge to take the necessary steps to deepen our prayer lives that we may be closer to God. What do you need to do to make this a realistic possibility?

One of the first things you may have to decide in praying with St Luke is this: are you the kind of person who keeps everything very private, and does not let it be seen? Or are you able to speak about your faith, and what it means to you? If you are in a group for the first time and feel shy about speaking out, you do have a right to begin slowly. First, get in touch with your feelings, and allow yourself to talk about them to God. How do you feel about being asked by God to allow his Son to come to live within you? Do you find it frightening, or do you feel the need like Mary to praise the Lord in thanksgiving? If you can share it with others, good. But be gentle with yourself. As we go through the gospel, you will grow in confidence. Just ask yourself this: if Elizabeth hadn't spoken out first, 'Blessed are you among women, and blessed is the fruit of your womb' (1:42), would Mary at that moment have given voice to her joy in the Lord? Of course the Holy Spirit had something to do with it. But the Spirit works through people.

4. RESPONSE

This is in many ways the most important part of our prayer. Your reflection has raised things you need to pray about. Your response must be personal. Respond to your own feelings of being blessed. Praise God in your own words for sending his Son, for Mary's lovely response of willingness and joy, which inspires us, and for the blessings you are becoming more and more aware of as you pray. Take time, if you are not used to thinking like this. It is all right to make short ejaculatory prayers, which come from the heart. Thank God for the gift of life you received from your parents, the love and care they were able to

give you, your baptism, the gifts of the Spirit, your friends, perhaps marriage, children, perhaps ordination, the eucharistic
presence, and so on. Above all, thank God for the gift of his
Beloved Son, and for making us his beloved sons and daughters.
Say the *Magnificat* in Mary's name, then in your own name. You
might try to make up (and write down) your own *Magnificat*,
praising God for your personal reasons; even something simple:
'God our Father, I praise and thank you with all my heart for all
your blessings, because ... because ... because ...' Thank God for
his goodness, mercy, love, imagination, creativity. Ask the Holy
Spirit's help to pray with the word of God, and for his inspiration that you may be able to speak out your faith and share it
with others, if only by a smile on your face and a ready welcome.

5. CONTEMPLATION

Do not be intimidated by the big word! Simply allow the 'mind-
set' you have fostered by your prayer to stay with you as you go
about your daily routines, and return to it in moments of quiet.
Choose a phrase from the *Magnificat* to repeat to yourself often;
e.g., 'The Mighty One has done great things for me.' We have the
example of Mary for this: 'Mary treasured all these words and
pondered them in her heart' (2:19, see also 1:66). When you live
with something, it becomes a part of you, and the Holy Spirit is
able to fill your heart with loving thoughts in a way that is often
surprising. It is the Spirit, after all, who has inspired the word of
God.

Prayer: Lord, give us a reflective spirit, that we may treasure
your words in our hearts, like Mary, and learn to say yes to your
will.

Review: Think about the process we have been using

Look back over the stages of our prayer: *Focus, Familiarisation* (careful reading and Background), *Reflection, Response, Contemplation*. We will use these stages with selected passages on our journey through Luke's gospel. The text of each passage chosen will be set out in a loosely structured way, using the NRSV. Some background will be given for each passage. Ideas will be proposed to stimulate your own reflection, using the suggested Key Words (see introduction pp 11-14) to aid your prayerful reading of the text. More time may have to be spent at the stage of *Reflection*, but you have not prayed with the text until you have made your personal *Response*. The most important part is your own attention to the text, your involvement with it, so that you may come to love and treasure the word of God, and seek to be nourished by it. The reflections offered are to stimulate your own thoughts and feelings, and are in no way to be seen as restrictive. The Holy Spirit will be your guide, if you are open to his inspiration.

Think of yourself beginning an adventurous journey with St Luke, with a mixture of excitement and trepidation, as we begin any adventure. Luke in Acts (9:2 etc.) refers to Christianity as 'the way', and we are going to walk 'the way' with the people of St Luke's gospel. We ask them to allow us to be part of their story, and invite them to be part of ours.

Session 2: Annunciation (Luke 1:26-38)

1. FOCUS
Focus the mind and heart on God's presence. For suggestions see Introduction (p 18), or Session 1 (p 26).

Prayer (based on Luke 1:4):
> God our Father, send us your Spirit,
> to open our hearts to the truth of the gospel.
> We believe in Jesus, your Beloved Son.
> We would like to know him better,
> to deepen our faith in him and our love for him.
> Help us through listening to Luke to earn the name
> Theophilus or Theophila, and become 'Lovers of God'.

2. FAMILIARISATION
Read slowly (preferably aloud) the story of the Annunciation, Luke 1:26-38. Read it as often as it takes to become familiar with the sequence of ideas/events in the passage. Close your eyes and retell the story to yourself, then look at the text to see what you have missed.

The Angel's Greeting
1:26 In the sixth month the angel Gabriel was sent by God
   to a town in Galilee called Nazareth,
27 to a virgin engaged to a man whose name was Joseph, of the house of David.
The virgin's name was Mary.
28 And he came to her and said, 'Greetings, favoured one! The Lord is with you.'
29 But she was much perplexed by his words
   and pondered what sort of greeting this might be.

The Wonderful Message
30 The angel said to her, 'Do not be afraid, Mary,
   for you have found favour with God.
31 And now, you will conceive in your womb and bear a son,
   and you will name him Jesus.
32 He will be great, and will be called Son of the Most High,

and the Lord God will give to him the throne of his ancestor
David.
33 He will reign over the house of Jacob forever,
and of his kingdom there will be no end.'

Reassurance
34 Mary said to the angel, 'How can this be, since I am a virgin?'
35 The angel said to her, 'The Holy Spirit will come upon you,
and the power of the Most High will overshadow you;
therefore the child to be born will be holy;
he will be called Son of God.

A Sign
36 And now, your relative Elizabeth in her old age has also conceived a son;
and this is the sixth month of her who was said to be barren.
37 For nothing will be impossible with God.'

Saying Yes to God's Plan
38 Then Mary said, 'Here am I, the servant of the Lord;
let it be with me according to your word.'
Then the angel departed from her.

2.1 Background
*Background information will be offered for each session. Recommended
procedure is to read the text first, note things that you would like to
know more about, pick out things that strike you as important. Then
read this background material before the Reflection stage, whether pri-
vately or in a group setting. It is especially important that group leaders be familiar with it beforehand. Read the text again in the light of
this background.*

2.1.1 *Structure of Luke's Infancy Narrative:* Luke's narrative of the
birth and early years of Jesus has a deliberate symmetry: an
introduction and a conclusion, with two annunciation stories
followed by a journey/revelation story, and two birth stories
followed by a journey/revelation story. At some stage an extra
journey/revelation story was added (the finding in the temple),
followed by a second conclusion (2:41-52).

Introduction (prologue) 1:1-4
Annunciation to Zechariah 1:5-25
Annunciation to Mary 1:26-38
          Visitation to Elizabeth 1:39-56
Birth of John the Baptist 1:57-80
Birth of Jesus 2:1-20
          Presentation in the Temple 2:21-38
Conclusion 1: 2:39-40
[Finding in the Temple 2:41-51
Conclusion 2: 2:52]

2.1.2 Annunciation Stories: Luke was familiar with annunciation and birth stories in the First [Old] Testament, which helped him to shape his narratives. Watch out for such stories in the Lectionary leading up to Christmas: Emmanuel, Isaiah 7:10-14 (Advent Sunday 4A and 20 December), birth of Samson, Judges 13:2-7, 24-25 (19 December), birth of Samuel, 1 Samuel 1:24-28 (22 December). They commonly include an angelic message, the mission of the child, a name, a request for reassurance, and a sign.

2.1.3 Mary was betrothed to Joseph the carpenter. Such betrothal was a more binding obligation than engagement nowadays. It was virtually an exchange of consent to marriage that only required the bridegroom formally to take the bride into his house to validate it. There is speculation that Mary, like other young Jewish women, might have dreamed of being the mother of the expected Messiah of the line of David. Some Catholic writers also speculate that Mary had already taken a vow of virginity, which seems very unlikely for a newly betrothed woman. Mary may have belonged to the tribe of Levi (admittedly a conclusion from her relationship to Elizabeth, the wife of the priest Zechariah), but Joseph was of the tribe of David. Through Joseph's formal acceptance of Jesus as his son, he belongs to the tribe of David. Other questions may arise, for which it may be necessary to consult commentaries. For our purposes, try to concentrate on what the passage tells us.

2.1.4 Israel's hope for a Messiah of the line of David: there were different lines of expectation among the Jews of Jesus' time, but the most common belief was that God would restore the line of King David by sending a Messiah (an anointed one, since kings were anointed). A promise had been made to David that there would always be one of his line on the throne (2 Samuel 7:11-16), but the Davidic kingship did not survive the Babylonian Exile (6th Century BC). Hope grew up that some day God would restore the royal line of David by raising up an ideal king who would accomplish God's will and reign for ever. Read 1:32-33: 'He will be great, and will be called Son of the Most High, and the Lord God will give to him the throne of his ancestor David. He will reign over the house of Jacob for ever, and of his kingdom there will be no end.' Imagine the excitement those words would cause to Mary or any Jew of the time.

2.1.5 Incarnation is the technical word for the eternal Son of God taking human flesh (*caro* is Latin for flesh) in the womb of Mary. It is important to note that the promised child fulfils the hopes for a Messiah of the line of David, but goes far beyond them. Luke wishes to convey the Christian faith in the unique Sonship of Jesus in the full sense, while knowing that at the time of the Incarnation, there was no knowledge of the doctrine of the Trinity, which allows us to say that the Father sent his eternal divine Son to take human flesh from Mary. That doctrine can only be properly grasped after the death and resurrection of Jesus, and the coming of the Holy Spirit. So Luke calls the child 'Son of the Most High' and 'Son of God', terms which can be understood in the full Christian sense, but at the time would have suggested the title of the kings of Israel, who were called 'son of God' because they represented the people before God. We just do not know what Mary or Joseph were able to understand about Jesus' divinity at the time, and perhaps we should not presume to know. Luke will conclude his gospel with explicit recognition of Jesus' true nature by the disciples: 'They worshipped him' (24:52) – see Session 21.

3. REFLECTION
Take a period of quiet to listen to what God may be saying to you through this text. In group work, the leader may invite those who feel

comfortable with it to share their initial thoughts on the passage (it is as important to listen to others as to talk!)

3.1 Journey: (May be omitted on this occasion if desired.) St Bernard pictures the world as waiting with baited breath for Mary to give her 'Yes', so that the great process of salvation may begin. Jesus 'comes down' from heaven to take flesh in the womb of Mary. Mary, having received the sign of Elizabeth's pregnancy, will set out on a journey to visit Elizabeth, a journey symbolic of the bearer of the Messiah bringing him to others. A traditional piety sees Mary as the 'Ark of the Covenant', the tent carried by the Israelites on their journey to the Holy Land, containing the tablets of the Law, later housed in the Holy of Holies in the temple, the place where God dwelt with his people. Mary is the God-bearer in two senses: she will give birth to the Son of God, and she brings him to Elizabeth, symbolically to the world. Each of us shares in our own way in the duty and privilege of bringing Jesus to others, as Mary brought him to Elizabeth. We have received a precious gift, to be treasured, the life of the Risen Christ within us, and it is not just for ourselves, but to be shared with others.

3.2 Joy: There is a gladness and thankfulness running through all Luke's infancy narrative, in spite of the occasional shadows of future suffering. Either individually, or in groups at the discretion of group leaders, it would be helpful to make a list of the reasons which give us joy in this story:
Some suggestions:
- this is the beginning of our salvation;
- the fulfilment of all God's promises to his People is now at hand;
- Mary is a very specially chosen one, 'favoured one' [or 'graced one'], who has 'found favour with God';
- her son will be 'Son of the Most High', the Messiah of the line of David, who will be a king whose kingdom will never end;
- the Holy Spirit, the creative power of God, will form the child in Mary's womb;
- Mary is perplexed, but ready and willing to listen, to say yes;
- Incarnation takes place when Mary says yes to God's plan.

Imagine yourself as Mary or any Jew of that time, and the dawning realisation coming upon you of the marvellous news brought by the angel. What are your feelings at this time? Do you feel joy arising in your heart? Gratitude? What are the reassuring things for Mary in the words of the angel that would help her to undertake the mission with courage? Would some of those reassurances be relevant to us too?

3.3 *Personal*: Ask the question: In what ways is this a personal message, firstly to Mary, secondly, to me/us at this time (see it addressed to you as Theophilus/a, 1:3-4)?

Mary is suddenly immersed in a new and very intimate relationship with God the Father, affirmed as 'favoured one', who is offered God's protective presence in a special way: 'The Lord is with you'; 'Do not be afraid.' The angel gives her the wonderfully exciting and frightening message that she is to be the mother of the Messiah. How? When she is understandably perplexed and troubled, she is given the reassurance that 'the Holy Spirit will overshadow you'. A sign is given to her: her cousin Elizabeth is also to have a child. Mary would have been aware of the call of prophets, and the promise of divinely commissioned children from the scriptures. She makes a personal and whole-hearted response, 'I am God's servant. Let it be so.' It is probably unwise to try to enter Mary's frame of mind at this moment, but we have her words from the *Magnificat* already: her consciousness of being chosen, her joy in the Lord, her sense that this choice will be momentous – 'All generations will call me blessed, for the Mighty One has done great things for me.' Mothers will be able to empathise with Mary in her mother's relationship with her child: Mary's pregnancy will set up a new intimacy not just between herself and her child, but between the Son of God and all humanity. Non-believers will always find the reality of the union between the divine and the human, which leaves both still truly themselves, hard to credit. For believers, we simple rejoice in the tremendous love of God for his people that urges him to send his Eternal Son to take flesh in the womb of Mary. Spend a little time reflecting on the wonder of the Incarnation.

How has this great message changed my/our personal relationship with God, with the Son of Mary, with the people of

God? Do you feel that it has made a big difference to your life? Through the Incarnation, we are called to an intimate relationship with God our Father, with Jesus, with the Holy Spirit. We may be carrying some baggage from previous relationships or images of God, and like Mary, we may feel initially frightened of too close a relationship with Jesus or God the Father. So it will help us to grow into these relationships if we look at the words of the angel and ask in what way they could apply to each of us. Do I think that the angel Gabriel could possibly be bringing a spiritual message for me now?

- Would the angel greet me with *'rejoice'*? Would Gabriel be wishing me personal joy at the coming of the Messiah?
- Would he call me *'favoured (i.e., graced) one'*? Yes, I am baptised into Christ, have the gifts of the Holy Spirit, with all the other graces and blessings I have received during my life.
- *'Do not be afraid'*: Can I admit to my personal worries and fears, and believe that God wants me to lay them aside? God is calling me to intimacy with himself through Jesus; the call is to me, not just to the saints.
- Could Christ be born in me? Well, of course, not historically as in Mary, but yes, spiritually, he wants to come live in me. 'Those who love me will keep my word, and my Father will love them, and we will come to them and make our home with them' (John 14:23). Do I want to say with Peter, 'Depart from me, for I am a sinful person, Lord' (Luke 5:8)? The Holy Spirit can be creative in me too. How do I feel about the possibility of having a rich inner life through the power of Jesus' birth, death and resurrection?

3.4 Challenge: We can certainly understand the challenge to Mary. With her 'Yes', Mary commits herself to a journey of doing God's will, which will lead her to ultimate joy through a difficult road filled with highs and lows she can only suspect now. Her journey will be in love for her son, and closely twinned with his fate and his mission. That is what will give the journey its meaning.

The challenge to me is the same on a lesser scale. I have to accept that I am graced, blessed with a living relationship with Jesus, and that I am called to walk with him wherever it may lead me; that he will help me to do the will of God, and that I will learn God's plan for me from his lips, from his relationship to the Father, and from his actions. The journey promises much joy, tough decisions, and staying power, otherwise known as fidelity. I will need to be full of faith, faithful.

4. RESPONSE

Pray quietly in your own words, responding to the joy that the beginning of the adventure of salvation brings to us all. Give thanks for the coming of the Son of God, for his taking flesh in the womb of Mary. What blessings are to come to us as a result of this special moment in history! It began then with Mary's 'Yes', it continues now in us. Express gratitude to God. God tells us not to be afraid, though we may be inclined to worry about the challenges to us in our following of Christ. Admit your worries; ask for grace to respond to what God asks of us, and to walk this journey, saying yes with courage like Mary. 'Lord, I want to make this journey. Help me to learn, to stay close to you, and not to lose heart.'

5. CONTEMPLATION

It is a good thing to pick out a phrase or sentence that speaks to you and repeat it slowly until you feel you can keep it with you all day, e.g., 'The Lord is with you.' Saying the Angelus is a good way to reflect prayerfully on the Annunciation to Mary and the Incarnation of Jesus. Everything we see around us is filled with his presence, because the Word of God became dust-of-the-earth flesh in the womb of Mary.

Prayer: Christ be beside me, Christ be before me, Christ be behind me, King of my heart. Christ be within me, Christ be below me, Christ be above me, never to part.

Session 3: The Birth of Jesus (Luke 2:1-20)

1. FOCUS

Focus the mind and heart on the presence of the Lord. In group sessions the leader welcomes the group and helps them to relax and quieten their minds. For suggestions see Introduction p 18, or Session 1 p 26.

Prayer (based on 2:10-11):

> Lord, we welcome the good news announced by your angels to the shepherds – news of great joy for all of us, that a Saviour has been born for us, who is Christ the Lord. Give us confidence in approaching your good news in St Luke's gospel. May we find there the joy that Jesus brings to us, ponder the good news, come to know our Saviour better, and be ready to tell the good news to others. We ask this through Christ our Lord. Amen

2. FAMILIARISATION

Read the passage until you are familiar with it. It is so well-known that you need to read it with fresh eyes. Note the suggested headings, and the phrases which Luke repeats – the text was intended to be heard. Luke repeats three times 'lying in a manger', twice with 'wrapped in bands of cloth' and calls it a sign. A sign points to something else more important: it is mysterious, and may point to Jesus laid in the tomb wrapped in bands of cloth (the saviour).

Introduction: Journey to Bethlehem, the city of David.

2:1 In those days a decree went out from the Emperor Augustus that all the world should be registered.

2 This was the first registration,

and was taken while Quirinius was governor of Syria.

3 All went to their own towns to be registered.

4 Joseph also went from the town of Nazareth in Galilee to Judea, to the city of David called Bethlehem, because he was descended from the house and family of David.

5 He went to be registered with Mary,

to whom he was engaged, and who was expecting a child.

The Birth of Jesus

6 While they were there, the time came for her to deliver her child.

7 And she gave birth to her firstborn son and
wrapped him in bands of cloth, and laid him in a manger,
because there was no room for them in the inn.

Revelation of its meaning

8 In that region there were shepherds living in the fields,
keeping watch over their flock by night.

9 Then an angel of the Lord stood before them, and the glory
of the Lord shone around them, and they were terrified.

10 But the angel said to them, 'Do not be afraid, for, see –
I am bringing you good news of great joy for all the people:

11 to you is born this day in the city of David a Saviour,
who is the Messiah [the Christ], the Lord.

12 This will be a sign for you: you will find a child
wrapped in bands of cloth and lying in a manger.'

13 And suddenly there was with the angel a multitude of the
heavenly host, praising God and saying,

14 'Glory to God in the highest heaven,
and on earth peace among those whom he favours.'

Responding: hearing, seeing, telling, pondering, praising.

15 When the angels had left them and gone into heaven,
the shepherds said to one another, 'Let us go now to Bethlehem
and see this thing that has taken place,
which the Lord has made known to us.'

16 So they went with haste and found Mary and Joseph,
and the child lying in the manger.

17 When they saw this, they made known what had been told
them about this child;

18 and all who heard it were amazed
at what the shepherds told them.

19 But Mary treasured all these words
and pondered them in her heart.

20 The shepherds returned, glorifying and praising God
for all they had heard and seen, as it had been told them.

2.1 Background
Group leaders need to be familiar with this background; others are encouraged to read it before attempting to pray with the text.

2.1.1 *The Messiah and the Romans:* When Jesus was born, the Romans ruled Judea through its subject king, Herod the Great (a Jew from Idumea, [Edom], educated in Rome), under the supervision of the Roman Governor of Syria. The census ordered by the Emperor Augustus involves difficult historical problems (if desired, consult a commentary). By divine providence it brings Joseph and Mary to Bethlehem, the town of David, where Jesus is born. The Messiah (Anointed One), of the line of David, was expected to restore the Davidic kingship and bring peace and blessings to God's people. How the Messiah would deal with the Roman occupation was obviously an area for debate, exaggerated hopes, and much confusion, and it was certainly a problem for Herod the Great. All shades of opinion were represented, from the Zealots who were ready to rebel against Rome, to the Sadducees – the Priest leaders – who feared any rocking of the boat. Group leaders should remember not to foster the impression that there were no spiritual expectations about the Messiah, as well as political ones.

2.1.2 *Geographical note:* Bethlehem was the town of Jesse, the place where David herded sheep as a boy and was anointed as future kind by Samuel. Matthew 2:5-6 quotes (with some paraphrase) the prophecy of Micah 5:1 (5:2 in NRSV) that out of Bethlehem would come 'the one who is to rule over Israel'. Luke makes no explicit reference to the prophecy, but takes the Davidic background for granted, and may have had David the shepherd in mind when the revelation by the angel is made to the shepherds. In Judea there is much porous limestone, which dissolves in water and allows many caves to be formed in the sides of hills (pilgrims are taken to the Shepherds' Field near Bethlehem to see examples). The caves offered shelter for animals in winter and coolness in summer, and were used as annexes to houses. The place where the birth of Jesus is commemorated is a grotto under the Basilica of the Nativity in Bethlehem, where there is a series of connected caves, which may be visited. St

Jerome lived there when in Bethlehem. Strictly speaking, Luke makes no mention of a cave, or of any animals therein, but it seems reasonable to suppose that they found an animal shelter of some sort, because of the threefold mention of the manger, and a limestone cave would be the most likely. The cave is first mentioned in a later non-canonical source, the *Protoevangelium of James*.

2.1.3 The Manger: Luke's emphasis on the manger as a sign is not easily interpreted. For the shepherds it was a way of locating the scene of the birth, but Luke seems to be conveying a deeper significance for the reader. Fitzmeyer (Vol 1, p 410) says the sign 'is an unusual one, corresponding in no way to the signs that one might have expected of a coming Messiah'. Alleged First Testament references are not very convincing, and there is perhaps more credibility in the suggestion of Hebblethwaite that the manger was a ledge or shelf in the limestone wall of the cave, rather than our concept of a wooden structure, reinforced by centuries of art and preaching. Luke repeats the words 'wrapped in bands of cloth and lying in a manger', because he is thinking forward to the next time Jesus is wrapped in 'bands of cloth' and laid on a ledge cut out of rock – in the tomb. Luke uses the word 'saviour' of Jesus in the angelic message to the shepherds (2:11), the only time Jesus is called 'saviour' in the first three gospels. Even as Luke proclaims his birth, he may be thinking of his death to save his people. The Christian message is built into the angel's proclamation: Jesus is Saviour, Messiah and Lord. It is a message of great joy for all the people: '[because] to you is born this day in the city of David a Saviour, who is the Messiah, the Lord'.

2.1.4 The Virgin Birth: We are engaged primarily on a prayerful reading of Luke to let the word nourish our spirits. Leaders are encouraged to steer away from intellectual discussions, but questions do arise. The Virgin Birth means that Jesus is conceived without a human father, through the creative power of the Holy Spirit. It does not mean that his actual birth is any more miraculous than the birth of any baby. Modern people are sceptical of miracles, but remember that we are dealing here with the divine, the wondrous, the unique Son of God. It is for us to learn from what God is doing, not to question his way of bringing about our salvation. No statement is being made that questions the goodness of normal human parenthood. The conception of Jesus is something totally unique.

3. REFLECTION

Take a period of quiet reflection. Imitate Mary, treasuring these words and pondering them in her heart (2:19). In group reflection, the group leader may invite a brief sharing of initial impressions. This may help others to get involved in the story. Listening is as important as talking.

3.1 *Journey:* Mary and Joseph make a difficult journey to Bethlehem. In the ancestral city they find no lodging; the 'Son of David' will be born like a refugee in David's home-town, thereby identifying with all homeless and marginalised people, as he will do throughout the gospel. We are used to having the scene prettified in Christmas cards, and while Luke puts no explicit emphasis on the poverty of Jesus' birth, the reality was probably pretty stark and very unhygienic. God has been preparing for this birth for hundreds of years, and when it comes the child of destiny is born in an animal shelter. We are reminded that God does not put much importance on a grand house or plush surroundings; the important thing for Jesus' welfare is the love of Mary and Joseph. Mary's maternal care is shown: she 'wrapped him in bands of cloth' as every mother did with her child in those days. For the shepherds, there is a shorter journey, but it is a real pilgrimage to a holy place from which they return much changed. 'They made known what had been told them about this child' (v 17); 'The shepherds returned glorifying and praising God for all that they had seen, as it had been told them' (v 20). People have been coming to Bethlehem ever since, thousands of pilgrims. We come in pilgrimage in our hearts to see, like the shepherds, to listen, to ponder, to praise and thank God for this birth, and to tell what we have discovered.

3.2 *Joy:* Luke sets the scene skilfully: the Roman empire is controlled by the Emperor Augustus, who as the adopted son of Julius Caesar was declared to be *divi filius* (son of a god; Julius had been deified by the Senate of Rome). On his proclamation the small people of the provinces move to be listed in their ancestral towns, and in the inconvenience of the journey Mary's child is born – treated in two low key verses. And unexpectedly, to unlikely people, there is a glorious proclamation from heaven of news that will bring joy to the people of the earth. The child laid in a manger is declared to be Saviour, Messiah, Lord, and a host of angels sing in glorious chorus: 'Glory to God in the highest heaven, and on earth peace among those whom he favours' (v 14). The angels add to the series of glad canticles in the early chapters of Luke praising and glorifying God. The shepherds, initially frightened, end up 'praising and glorifying God for all they had heard and seen' (v 20). So the joy of this passage cannot be suppressed, and we must make it our own. Go through the text quietly (alone or in a group) and list the reasons why we should read this story with glad hearts. We have seen some of them already: e.g., 'good news of great joy for all the people' (10), 'to you is born a saviour' (11); 'glory to God,' 'peace on earth,' (14) the shepherds 'returned glorifying and praising God' (20). So then, as we say in the Mass, 'Lift up your hearts!' and allow yourself to experience the joy of the birth of our Saviour, the real Son of God, who will bring peace that will surpass that of the *pax Romana*, the peace of the Roman empire. We have heard this good news so often that we have forgotten what it must have been like to hear it for the first time. Listen to it again in your heart and be glad.

3.3 *Personal:* In what ways does Luke present this as a personal message? For the actors in the story? For us?

What are the personal reactions of the people in the story? Strangely, Luke concentrates much more on the reactions of the shepherds that on those of Mary and Joseph. Nothing is said about Joseph's reactions, though we may speculate about his concern for Mary and the child, his attempts to protect and ease their situation – no man is too happy that he cannot provide the best accommodation for his wife and child. Mary's maternal care is indicated briefly, but nothing is said about her feelings for the child and the tremendous responsibilities facing her; just that she listened to the shepherds' story and 'treasured all these words and pondered them in her heart'. Mary and Joseph teach us to trust in God, to be content with what God gives us, to rejoice in the right things, to treasure and ponder the word of God. It seems strange that the revelation of the meaning of the event is to the shepherds, not to Mary and Joseph. Perhaps the shepherds represent us? Think of the sequence of reactions by the shepherds: at first they are afraid, but they listen to the astonishing message, then decide to act, to go and see, then they find it is all as they have been told, so they tell the story to others, and praise the Lord. Read the words of the angel again, and see them as addressed to you personally: 'to *you* is born this day ... a Saviour!' Through the shepherds the meaning is revealed to us also, and action suggested. We are called to be witnesses in those two senses, to go and see (gaze and think about the meaning of the scene), and go and tell others what we have discovered. As you become more conscious of being called by God to a deeper and more personal relationship, you may find yourself going through the same stages as the shepherds: being afraid, becoming aware of the wonder of the message, deciding to act, experiencing the joy of involvement, telling others, and glorifying and praising God for all you have seen and heard.

3.4 Challenge: Mary and Joseph are challenged to do God's will in difficult circumstances. They go on a journey which seems to have a poor end, but really has a wonderful outcome. They provide the child with love and protection. They listen and ponder: there are hints that being born in a stable is not the only or the most alarming thing in this child's destiny. They seem to face the future with serene faith.

The shepherds are challenged to fear not, to believe the incredible good news, to take action – go and see, to find the child, to spread the news by telling others, to share their joy, to praise the Lord. They are examples of the spontaneous faith and joy that we find in Luke's gospel.

Challenge to us? We are not Mary and Joseph, but we can do some things they did. We are called to believe in this vulnerable child who is Son of God and Son of Mary. We are called to put our trust in God's way of doing things, even when we'd like to tell God we could arrange things better. If we treasure the word and ponder it, it may help us not to treasure the wrong things. As we think of the eternal Son of God putting himself totally in the hands of Mary and Joseph, we may learn to respect Jesus in his Body: 'Whatever you do to one of these ... you do to me.' The shepherds really challenge us. 'Little people' hear the good news with some fear, but great joy, act on it, believe, spread the good news, praise God with joy. That is a lifetime of challenges for us. We need to look for the courage to respond.

4. RESPONSE

It is a wonderful story, and we need to respond in prayer of praise from the heart. Spend some time quietly gazing at the scene on which we have been reflecting. Be still if you can; if you need words, try repeating the titles of Jesus: Saviour, Messiah, Lord, Son of God, Son of Mary. Thank God for this birth. Bless the Lord for coming to us in this totally vulnerable state. Ask the Spirit in his creative power to let Jesus be born in our hearts, to help us to 'treasure all these words' and ponder them in our hearts. Like the shepherds, picture yourself hearing this unbelievable news, wondering could it be true, deciding to go and see, and being amazed, unable to stop talking about it. Our response is not to be just in words, but in action. What do we need to do to spread this news, to affirm others in their faith, to reassure doubters? Can we do that if we are not able to radiate joy in the coming of the Son of God among us? Jesus wants to share his joy with us: pray for it.

5. CONTEMPLATION

Live with this story in moments of quiet. Think again about choosing a text to ponder. St Francis of Assisi believed that the Incarnation made the most tremendous difference to everything in creation; the divinity is forever united to the clay of earth and to our human flesh, so everything is new through the presence of Jesus. This creates an awareness of the presence of the Lord in ourselves, in our brothers and sisters, and in all creation. Carry this awareness with you. Have a phrase to repeat to yourself often: 'To you is born this day ... a Saviour, who is the Messiah, the Lord'; or 'You will find a child wrapped in bands of cloth and lying in a manger'.

Prayer:
O come all ye faithful, joyful and triumphant,
O come ye, O come ye, to Bethlehem.
Come and adore him, born the king of angels;
O come let us adore him,
O come let us adore him,
O come let us adore him, Christ the Lord.

Firmly I believe and truly
God is three and God is one.
And I next acknowledge duly,
Manhood taken by the Son.
And I hope and trust most fully
In that manhood crucified,
And each thought and deed unruly
Do to death as he has died.
(Cardinal Newman)

Session 4: The Baptism of Jesus (Luke 3:21-22)

1. FOCUS
Spend some time focusing your body and mind on the presence of God. For suggestions see Introduction p 18, or Session 1 p 26.

Prayer:
> Father, prepare us to hear Luke's words about the baptism of Jesus in the river Jordan. You spoke to Jesus as your beloved Son, and filled his humanity with your Spirit, that he might begin his mission. Help us to listen as your sons and daughters. Fill us with your Spirit that we may learn about Jesus' mission, and the call that our baptism gives to us. We ask this through Christ our Lord. Amen.

2. FAMILIARISATION
Read the text carefully a few times until familiar with it. This text of Luke is short: close your eyes and tell it to yourself. It may take more than one go.
> 3:21 Now when all the people were baptised,
> and when Jesus also had been baptised and was praying,
> the heaven was opened,
> 22 and the Holy Spirit descended upon him
> in bodily form like a dove.
> And a voice came from heaven,
> 'You are my Son, the Beloved; with you I am well pleased.'

2.1 Background
This material must be read beforehand by those who act as group leaders, and by others if possible. Leaders should encourage participants in group study to read Luke 3:1-20 about John the Baptist before studying the baptism of Jesus, and to read the Background before coming to a group session.

2.1.1 John the Baptist: Luke gives us more information about John the Baptist than Mark or Matthew. He begins from the same text as Mark and Matthew, the prophecy of Isaiah chapter 40, about preparing 'the way of the Lord'. Isaiah chapters 40-55 is addressed to the exiles in Babylon in the 6th century BC, promising them a new deliverance (*exodus*, lit. journey out) from exile to their own land, like the first exodus from slavery in Egypt. Using this text, John the Baptist points to another saving action of God, a third exodus, which will save humanity from slavery to sin and bring them to the freedom of the children of God. Only Luke in the transfiguration story (9:28-36) will speak of Jesus discussing his own exodus in Jerusalem, his passing from this life to the Father. We will see when we come to that passage that we are all called to follow Jesus on that 'journey out'. The Baptist points to the More Powerful One who is to come after him, who will baptise with 'Holy Spirit and fire'. In Luke's style of writing, he often finishes what he has to say about one person before going on to the next, so he has John arrested by Herod (Antipas) before beginning the baptism of Jesus. Therefore he does not say who baptised Jesus.

2.1.2 Echoes of important passages from the First Testament: Most commentators see in 3:22 deliberate echoes of the following two texts:

Psalm 2:7 (A royal messianic psalm, which originally referred to the coronation of kings of David's line, then to the longed for Messiah of the line of David. The words of the Father to Jesus, 'You are my Son', suggest this whole line of thought):
I will tell of the decree of the Lord:
He said to me, 'You are my son; today I have begotten you.'

Isaiah 42:1 (The first Song of the Suffering Servant of God, believed by Jewish teachers to refer to Israel in general and not to the Messiah. The echoes here are to the ideas rather than the words, but in the Greek translation of the text of Isaiah the word for 'servant', *pais*, can also mean 'son', 'delights' is synonymous with 'well pleased', and the Spirit is given in both passages):
Here is my servant, whom I uphold,
My chosen, in whom my soul delights;
I have put my spirit upon him ...

2.1.3 Jesus' Baptism: Jesus' baptism is presented as a vocation ('call') story, its shape based on call stories from the First Testament, in particular the call of a prophet (see the call of

Isaiah 6:1-8, or Jeremiah 1:1-10). Three elements are common: the opening of the heavens, indicating the presence of God; a divine message, giving a role and a mission (may include affirmation and reassurance); and the gift of the Spirit, giving the power to carry out the mission. These elements are present in the Baptism of Jesus. It is important therefore to see more than the affirming of the relationship of Sonship, important though that may be, in the Father's words to Jesus. The words of the Father also describe his mission, and call him to begin that mission. The reason we find this difficult to see is that we are not as familiar with key biblical texts as Jesus' contemporaries and the early Christians were. Texts associated with the expected Messiah rang immediate bells with them, and placing texts not associated with the Messiah beside them raised immediate questions. The Father's words to Jesus refer clearly to a well known Messianic text, Psalm 2:7, indicating that Jesus is to be the promised royal Messiah of the line of David (expected message). But they also allude to a text which had never been associated with the Messiah, Isaiah 42: 1-7, which is called the First Servant Song (one of a set of songs referring to a Suffering Servant of God who is rejected and dies a cruel death as a criminal) – a totally unexpected reference. Can this be Jesus' mission, to unite the roles of Messianic King and Suffering Servant? How can it be done? Understandably Jesus goes into the desert to reflect on his mission, and has to resist the devil's temptation to take the easy way.

3. REFLECTION

Take a period of quiet refection on the text. Luke says that Jesus was praying when this great experience took place. In a group, the leader may wish to invite the participants to share briefly what strikes them, and listen to others.

3.1 *Journey:* This is a turning point in the life of Jesus. Up to now he has been a member of a family at Nazareth, working as a small time contractor/carpenter. His growing realisation of the mission to which he is called is triggered by the preaching of John the Baptist. He journeys from Galilee to Judea, prayerfully accepts baptism from the Baptist, and finds himself receiving an

overwhelming call and mission. In our times a deeper understanding of the sacrament of baptism has led to a realisation that
through baptism we are also called to mission, sharing the mission of Christ, Priest, Prophet and King. With baptism we begin
a journey which may have many turnings, but whose goal is life
with God. A sense of being called can strike us too, when we
realise the great love God has for us, and what the coming of
Jesus means for us, overwhelming us with love and joy. Can you
identify any such experience in your life?

3.2 *Joy:* Is this good news for us? List points in the story which
should make us thankful, e.g., the Father's loving affirmation of
Jesus as his Son; the presence of Holy Spirit (when the doctrine
of the Trinity much later becomes clear, Christians rejoice in the
presence of Father, Son and Holy Spirit at this important moment in the mission of Jesus); this call marks the beginning of
Jesus mission for humanity; the dawning possibility that we,
who are baptised 'into Christ' are also God's beloved sons and
daughters filled with the Spirit.

Jesus' baptism was less and more than our Sacrament of
Baptism: less because the baptism of John was not the sacrament, which gives us a share in the life of the Risen Christ; more
because of the action of the Father and the outpouring of the
Holy Spirit upon him. Luke in Acts 10:38 has Peter say that 'God
anointed Jesus of Nazareth with the Holy Spirit and with
power.' Rejoice that Jesus will begin his mission in the power of
the Spirit, and that we share in the same Spirit through baptism
and confirmation.

3.3 *Personal:* How are the personal relationship of Jesus with his
Father and our relationship to the Father through Jesus illumin-
ated by this passage?
Jesus? It is almost impossible for us to comprehend how deeply
strengthening, comforting and affirming this experience was to
Jesus' humanity. Remember that he had a real human nature,
with a human need for affirmation and love.
- He is baptised, presumably by John, and is praying to God
  his Father.
- Then he has a beautiful intimate experience of Trinity, the
  Spirit comes upon him, the Father speaks to him.

- The words are intimate: 'You are my Son, the Beloved'. (In Matthew it is 'This is my Son.') He is recognised, loved, and affirmed by the Father, who is 'well pleased with him'.

Personal to me/us?

- We are baptised with a greater baptism than John's.
- So we are affirmed as God's sons and daughters;
- We receive the gifts of the Spirit in baptism and confirmation.
- Think of the Father's words as addressed to you. 'You are my son/daughter.' How does that make you feel? Think of an answer!

3.4 Challenge: Jesus is called to a very demanding mission. He was very familiar with the call of the prophets, and he recognised the moment: heaven opened, the power of the Holy Spirit comes upon him, the Father speaks words deeply consoling, but very challenging. He believed in the messianic understanding of Psalm 2:7 as God addressing the Messiah, 'You are my Son.' Now those words have been addressed to Jesus by God the Father. The implications are huge! The references to the Servant of God are less obvious, but they do seem to be there: the Spirit, the title 'Chosen' and 'Beloved' (both used as titles of the Messiah), the echo of 'my soul delights in you' in the words of the Father, 'I am well pleased with you.' His mission, then, is to combine the role of Messianic King with that of Servant. We have no idea how mind-shaking that was even to Jesus, who was taught by the Rabbis that the Suffering Servant Songs referred to Israel and had nothing to do with the Messiah. We begin to realise how difficult it will be for him to get his disciples to understand this, not to speak of those who opposed him. He needs to go into the desert on retreat to think this one through. Of course it will be a temptation, exploited by the devil, to take the popular way of kingly power rather than service. But Jesus has been affirmed in his identity, he knows who he is, and he has the power of the Holy Spirit in him to carry out his mission.

Challenge to us:
- To appreciate that baptism links us to Father, Son and Spirit.
- To realise that we are made children of God, loved by God.
- To know that this for us also involves a mission. At baptism

we all begin a journey. We share in Jesus' roles as prophet (called to witness), priest (called to pray), and king/servant (called to serve). How do we respond to the idea of having a mission? Can we carry it out in our daily ('ordinary') lives? What power has God given us to carry out our mission? Is there any one thing you might do to respond better to your baptismal call? Pray for courage.

4. RESPONSE

Try to respond personally in prayer to all you have been thinking about. Give thanks to God the Father for the call of Jesus, for his readiness to answer such a difficult call, for his example of prayer, and response to the Holy Spirit. Give praise to the Blessed Trinity, Father, Son and Holy Spirit, now for the first time being gradually revealed to humanity. Give thanks for your own baptism and confirmation, and for our own call to share the dignity and the mission of Jesus. Ask for the courage to use your gifts, to join with Jesus in his priestly work of praying for the salvation of all God's people, in offering the Eucharist to the Father, with the Son, in the Spirit; to join in Jesus' prophetic work by witnessing to him by our words and actions; to join in his kingly service by dedicating ourselves again 'to love and serve the Lord', and to serve one another. Rejoice in the conviction that you are God's beloved son or daughter, and that the Spirit of God gives you strength and power for everything to which God calls you. Ask the Spirit to renew his gifts within you.

5. CONTEMPLATION

It is important that you keep in mind your dignity as a beloved son or daughter of God. Let it bring a smile to your face every now and again! Think of Jesus, king and servant, or as priest, prophet and king. Remember that the Spirit fills you with gifts and the Father loves you. You know who you are! Keep the text alive in you, 'You are my son (daughter), the beloved.'

BLESSED BE THE LORD

Prayer:

Almighty, eternal God, when the Holy Spirit descended upon Jesus at his baptism in the Jordan, you revealed him as your own beloved Son, and called him to begin his mission. Keep us, your children born of water and the Spirit, faithful to our calling, through Jesus Christ our Lord. Amen.

Through him (Jesus), with him and in him, in the unity of the Holy Spirit, all glory and honour is yours, Almighty Father, for ever and ever. Amen.

Session 5: The Public Ministry Begins (Luke 4:14-30)

1. *Focus*

Take time, individually or in a group, to focus mind and heart on God's presence. For suggestions see Introduction p 18, or Session 1 p26.

Prayer: O God of truth, prepare our minds
To hear and heed your holy word;
Fill every heart that longs for you
With your mysterious presence, Lord.
(Office of Readings, Monday, week 1)

2. *Familiarisation*

Read the text until you become familiar with it; notice the sequence of events, the respect Jesus is given in the synagogue, his being asked to read the sacred words of scripture, then his dramatic comment on the text, and the initial goodwill turning to hostility.

Introduction
4:14 Then Jesus, filled with the power of the Spirit,
returned to Galilee, and a report about him
spread through all the surrounding country.
15 He began to teach in their synagogues,
and was praised by everyone.

Jesus announces in Nazareth the programme for his ministry
16 When he came to Nazareth, where he had been brought up,
he went to the synagogue on the sabbath day,
as was his custom. He stood up to read,
17 and the scroll of the prophet Isaiah was given to him.
He unrolled the scroll and found the place where it was written:
18 'The Spirit of the Lord is upon me,
because he has anointed me to bring good news to the poor.
He has sent me to proclaim release to the captives
and recovery of sight to the blind,
to let the oppressed go free,
19 to proclaim the year of the Lord's favour.' [Isaiah 61:1-2a]
20 And he rolled up the scroll, gave it back to the attendant,

and sat down.
The eyes of all in the synagogue were fixed on him.
21 Then he began to say to them,
'Today this scripture has been fulfilled in your hearing.'
22 All spoke well of him and were amazed
at the gracious words that came from his mouth.

'He came unto his own, his own received him not.' (John 1:11)
They said, 'Is not this Joseph's son?'
23 He said to them,
'Doubtless you will quote to me this proverb,
"Doctor, cure yourself."
And you will say, "Do here also in your hometown
the things that we have heard you did in Capernaum".'
24 And he said, 'Truly I tell you,
no prophet is accepted in the prophet's hometown.
25 But the truth is,
there were many widows in Israel in the time of Elijah,
when the heaven was shut up three years and six months,
and there was a severe famine over all the land;
26 yet Elijah was sent to none of them
except to a widow at Zarephath in Sidon. [1 Kings chap 17]
27 There were also many lepers in Israel
in the time of the prophet Elisha,
and none of them was cleansed
except Naaman the Syrian.' [2 Kings chap 5]
28 When they heard this
all in the synagogue were filled with rage.
29. They got up, drove him out of the town,
and led him to the brow of the hill
on which their town was built,
so that they might hurl him off the cliff.
30 But he passed through the midst of them
and went on his way.

2.1 *Background: Try to read the text and the background notes before coming to a group session. Group leaders should make themselves familiar with the material.*

2.1.1 *Context:* The previous episode is the testing of Jesus in the

THE PUBLIC MINISTRY BEGINS

desert, where he grappled with his vocation as Servant-Messiah. Jesus resists the devil's temptation to shirk the difficult side of his ministry, and returns to Galilee 'filled with the power of the Spirit' (v14). The devil departs for a time, to return later. The passion of Jesus will be presented by Luke as Jesus encountering 'the power of darkness' (22:53).

2.1.2 Luke does not follow Mark's order of events, and deliberately brings the episode at Nazareth to the beginning of the public ministry. It is clear that it was not the first thing to happen. He already had a reputation when he returned to Nazareth: 'You will say, do here in your hometown the things that we have heard you did in Capernaum' (4:23). Why does Luke change the order of events? He finds in this episode a programme for Jesus' ministry, and a glimpse of the whole ministry in miniature. Jesus presents his teaching, is at first well received, then opposition begins to grow, and (some of) his own people decide to kill him. Is not this what happened in the whole ministry?

2.1.3 *The Programme* is taken from Isaiah 61:1-2a. This belongs to the last part of the Book of Isaiah, and is material from a disciple of the original Isaiah, who belonged to the time after the Israelites returned to Jerusalem from exile in Babylon (6th century BC). Conditions were poor, and the prophet uses the ideal of the Jubilee Year, 'the year of the Lord's favour', to give them courage. The Jubilee was a concept that after 50 years all debts should be forgiven, captives set free, and property restored to rightful owners – a time of celebration and hope. Jesus proclaims a Jubilee, a time of liberation, restoration and hope, especially for the poor. His programme will not be just about social conditions, though those mattered immensely to him, but about freedom from spiritual slavery to sin, about forgiveness. Essentially he is referring in another way to the proclamation of the kingdom of God, which we find at the beginning of the public ministry in Mark and Matthew. Luke presents it as a Messianic programme: 'The Spirit of the Lord is upon me, because he has anointed me to bring good news to the poor.' The Messiah is the Anointed One, and Jesus says, 'Today this scripture has been fulfilled in your hearing.'

2.1.4 *The change of mood:* In a prayerful reading of the lengthy passage, time will dictate concentration on the first part with its initially favourable reception of the message of Jesus. There are several attempts to explain how the mood of the people abruptly swung from favourable to hostile, but in reality the evangelist does not give enough details, if he had them, to explain it all. Luke was a gentile, so he is able to highlight salvation offered to gentiles if the Jewish people reject it, as he witnessed in Acts. He used the references to the widow of Zarepath and Naaman the Syrian, both Gentiles (1 Kings 17 and 2 Kings 5). In miniature we have the whole story of Jesus, a preview of his coming rejection and death, and the gentile mission (most of Luke's community were probably gentile converts). We have to face the possibility of our own rejection of the message of Jesus. Indeed, how much of it have Christians failed or refused to implement, especially in regard to the poor?

2.1.5 *Jubilee Year:* Those who still remember the Jubilee Year 2000 remember that Pope John Paul II used this text of Luke as a programme for the renewal of the church. Writing about the coming Jubilee in 1994, he said: 'A Jubilee is always an occasion of special grace, a time of joy. The Jubilee of the year 2000 is meant to be a great prayer of praise and thanksgiving, especially for the gift of the Incarnation of the Son of God, and the redemption which he accomplished. In the Jubilee Year Christians will stand with the renewed wonder of faith before the love of the Father, who gave his Son "that whoever believes in him should not perish but have everlasting life".' (John 3:16) *Tertio Millennio Adveniente* (1994) 32.

3. REFLECTION
Take a period of quiet refection on the text. The group leader might like to draw it to a conclusion by inviting group members to share briefly the initial impact of the passage on their thinking. It is as important to listen as to talk.

3.1 *Journey:* Jesus has come home to begin his journey away from Nazareth, his public ministry. At the beginning of this great adventure, we are given a hint of how it will end (or seem to end), with his death. Later Luke will use the term 'exodus', and show it is a journey to life rather than death. Think what a jump in understanding the people of Nazareth are being asked to make: one who has lived among them for 30 years as a carpenter has gone away for a short period, then returns to proclaim himself Messiah and propose a programme from God. We are setting ourselves to follow Jesus on this journey through Luke, hoping to make his programme more and more our own, and we pray that he will bring us with him, and help us not to be discouraged by setbacks.

3.2 *Joy:* This is a proclamation of the good news, the promise of God's favour. It comes through the person of Jesus, who is identified as the 'anointed one' (Messiah), on whom the Spirit of the Lord has been poured out. Luke uses all his skill to focus our attention on the dramatic moment when Jesus sits down (the position of a teacher in Israel), and all eyes are fixed on him for the announcement, 'Today this scripture has been fulfilled in your hearing' (v 21). We rejoice for the poor, the unfree, and the blind. We rejoice for ourselves in so far as we feel our own poverty, the things that hold us captive, the darkness that is still inside us, the fears and hurts that keep us from being truly free. We may be slightly afraid even of this call to be free and to set free, and so conscious of our need for deliverance. Alas, many see their Christianity not as a freedom, but as a burden, a killjoy, and there may be remnants of that is ourselves. *Lord, free us from our slavery to fear and sin, and help us to know true freedom in you. Help us to learn from you how to share our lives with those who are in need.*

3.3 *Personal:* The message is a personal announcement of the good news to his own people in Nazareth, by Jesus who is conscious that he has been anointed 'to bring good news to the poor'. He must have wished with all his heart that his own people would receive the message gladly, and have been very disappointed that they turned against him and the message of deliverance. But he was familiar enough with the prophets to know that those who told the truth from God were badly received. His own people initially reacted well, and then allowed their own familiarity with him to put them off. Over familiarity with Christianity is one of the curses of the 21st century – it's all old hat, old fashioned. We need to rediscover our personal relationship with Jesus and the joy of his message of love and forgiveness. He is announcing a message not just for the people of Nazareth, but for me. Today this scripture is being fulfilled in my hearing as well. Am I listening? Are there bits of the message I would rather not think about? In the new millennium we have been called by the late Pope John Paul II to seek the face of Jesus, to get to know him personally.

3.4 *Challenge:* The challenge for Jesus is the realisation of his destiny and the mission he has to accomplish. He puts it forward with joy, and soon meets rejection. He is aware now of the difficulties he will face in his mission, and the awfulness of rejection. He does not flinch or mince his words. Jesus is 'filled with the power of the Spirit (v 14)'.

There is an immense challenge for me – to make the message my own; and for the church, to proclaim the message to the poor and the marginalised and to make it real by living it. The challenge is to keep hope alive in a world filled with injustice and division and conflict, where vulnerable people are exploited and enslaved for other people's profit. The challenge is to keep the flame of hope alive. We may not have power, but the challenge to us is to do small things to bring help to the poor and the afflicted. Are we ready for such a challenge?

4. RESPONSE

Give praise to God for sending his Son to proclaim his favour and mercy. Welcome this news in your heart. Thank God for his generous forgiveness, and his accepting love. Admit any problems we have in believing in it. It is hard to believe that we are totally loved, God's beloved sons and daughters. Admit our need of deliverance. Ask for release from fears, inhibitions, burdens that we drag about with us year after year and can not cut asunder. Ask pardon for the influence that this material and greedy world has upon us, that makes us look for possessions and status and worry about how other people perceive us. Renew our loyalty to Jesus and to his message and to his ways.

5. CONTEMPLATION

Put yourself mentally in the audience in the Synagogue at

Nazareth as Jesus makes his momentous announcement of God's love and graciousness to us. Try to keep an attitude of thankfulness for this in your heart, and live in the presence of that great good will from our God. Pick a text to remind you and repeat it often to yourself: e.g. 'The spirit of the Lord is upon me.' 'He has sent me to proclaim ... the Lord's year of favour.' 'Today this scripture has been fulfilled in your hearing.'

Prayer: Almighty Father, with your Son
      And blessed Spirit, hear our prayer:
      Teach us to love eternal truth
      And seek its freedom everywhere.
      (Office of Readings, Monday, wk 1)

Session 6: Call and Response:
Learning to be a disciple
(Luke 5:1-11)

1. FOCUS
Take time individually or in a group to focus mind and heart on the presence of God. See Introduction p 18, or Session 1 p 26 for suggestions.

Prayer:

> Jesus, we thank you for calling us to be your disciples. We praise you with Mary, Zechariah and Simeon for all your blessings. Give us the grace to meet you personally. Take away our fears, so that we may respond more generously to your personal call to us. Help us to be humble in your presence, but to know that we are accepted, healed and loved. In this knowledge, give us the courage to allow you to use us in your service. Amen.

2. FAMILIARISATION
Read the text a few times until you are familiar with the sequence of events. Try to identify with Simon Peter, and notice the stages by which he becomes involved (some suggestions are made in italics). He goes from being casual observer to committed disciple. Close your eyes and play the story over in your mind like a video.

Jesus the teacher

> 5:1 Once when Jesus was standing beside the lake of Gennesaret, and the crowd was pressing in on him to hear the word of God,
>
> 2 he saw two boats there at the shore of the lake;
> the fishermen had gone out of them and were washing their nets. *Uninvolved observer*
>
> 3 He got into one of the boats, the one belonging to Simon,
> *Personal meeting*
> and asked him to put out a little way from the shore.
> *Limited involvement*
> Then he sat down and taught the crowds from the boat.

Jesus the provider of amazing riches

    4 When he had finished speaking, he said to Simon,
    'Put out into the deep water   *Asking for more*
    and let down your nets for a catch.'
    5 Simon answered, 'Master, we have worked all night long
    but have caught nothing.   *Hesitation*
    Yet if you say so, I will let down the nets.'   *Respect*
    6 When they had done this, they caught so many fish
    that their nets were beginning to break,   *Astonishment*
    7 So they signalled their partners in the other boat to come
    and help them. And they came and filled both boats, so that
    they began to sink.

Jesus who calls and challenges.

    8 But when Simon Peter saw it, he fell down at Jesus' knees,
    saying, 'Go away from me, Lord, for I am a sinful man!'
                                       Awe, unworthiness
    9 For he and all those who were with him were amazed
    at the catch of fish they had taken;   *Salutary fear*
    10 and so also were James and John, sons of Zebedee, who
    were partners with Simon.
    Then Jesus said to Simon, 'Do not be afraid;   *Reassurance*
    from now on you will be catching people.'   *Hearing the call*

Discipleship

    11 When they had brought their boats to shore,
    they left everything and followed him.   *Commitment*

2.1 Background
Leaders of groups should be familiar with this background before begin-
ning to lead a session. All should try to read the background material
before beginning a new group session.

2.1.1 Luke's setting: In Mark (1:16-20) the call of the first disciples
comes immediately after the proclamation of the Kingdom of
God. They abruptly leave everything and follow Jesus (though
John Chapter One tells us they had been already disciples of the
Baptist and through him came to Jesus). Luke edits the text so
that Jesus has a fairly lengthy Galilean ministry before this calling of the first disciples. He has already healed Simon's mother-
in-law (4:38f), but Simon is named there as an unknown

Galilean, any mention of discipleship being edited out until the episode we are considering. So Simon has already seen Jesus' power at work and heard his words before he is challenged to become a disciple. This gives a better psychological explanation for Simon's (and his associates') decision to leave everything and follow Jesus (5:11).

2.1.2 The miraculous catch of fish (5:4-10): Luke includes in the call story the miracle of the fish, which resembles the post-resurrection story in John 21:4-11. A majority of commentators think they refer to the same incident, which came down to John and Luke as an isolated story, and they inserted it at different places in the narrative. There are indications in the Lucan narrative that it fits better after Easter. In v 8 Simon is called Simon Peter (all other references are to Simon), and Jesus is addressed as Lord, a post-resurrection term to signify his oneness with the Father. In addition, Simon's consciousness of unworthiness perhaps fits better after his denial of Jesus. But Luke has no resurrection appearances in Galilee, and Simon was called both before and after the resurrection, so he uses the story here.

2.1.3 The stages of Simon's call are illustrated by Luke, using all his skill as a storyteller. Simon has witnessed Jesus' power (the healing of his mother-in-law); he and his companions have heard Jesus teaching ('the word of God', 5:1), while cleaning their nets (uncommitted observers). Then Jesus addresses him personally, asking a favour, the use of his boat. Simon willingly agrees; it is the kind of challenge most of us can cope with. But he is soon further challenged to trust Jesus, he a fisherman to trust a carpenter about catching fish! He is to put out into deep water for a catch. He is sceptical at first: he would not expect to catch fish at this time. But he has too much respect for Jesus to refuse. So he is amazed at the catch of fish, then frightened, very conscious of his sinfulness in the presence of divine power. He allows himself to be reassured, finds acceptance, and the grace to commit himself to following Jesus. His example helps the others to decide.

2.1.4 As with all good stories, it is easy to universalise, to apply these stages to Jesus' call to any disciple, then or now. I have seen here the story of my own vocation to the priesthood, certainly in less dramatic form, but recognisably! Watching from a distance, listening, respecting, accepting small commitments, amazement when it becomes very personal, fear, a sense of unworthiness and sinfulness, reassurance, acceptance, commitment – watch out for these stages (or graces!) in your own life story.

3. REFLECTION
Take a period of silence to reflect on the text. The group leader may wish to end it by asking those who are comfortable with it to share briefly what initially strikes them about the passage. Others may prefer to listen.

3.1 *Journey:* Simon has been out in the boat all night, fruitlessly fishing. He is asked to go out again, and it makes all the difference. As the story unfolds, he is an interested but uninvolved observer, and is gradually drawn into the heart of Jesus' mission, leaving everything to follow Jesus on his journey. Jesus invites Simon and ourselves to become more than interested observers, to let him come close to us personally, to shed our fears and our sense of unworthiness, and to allow him to lead us. He does not need disciples who are worthy (who is?), just disciples who are willing to allow Jesus to work through them. Resolve to try to be open, in this journey through Luke's gospel, to the needs of your inner journey with Jesus. Compare your reactions to those of Simon.

3.2 *Joy:* Jesus is popular, spell-binding, attractive (drawing people to him). People want to be near him, some are willing to give themselves whole-heartedly to his call, even though frightened and feeling unworthy. We know that they will make mistakes, fail frequently, but they will come through in the end, with God's help. Jesus calls unlikely people, reaches out to you and me, patiently, gently, but with a quiet urgency. He gives in abundance, reassures us, accepts us with all our weakness and limitations. It is a source of joy that Jesus calls us to be members of God's people, part of the Body of Christ, sharing his priestly dignity through baptism, empowered by God's Holy Spirit. If you have been called to marriage, religious life, priesthood, or any of the other ministries in the church, give thanks for your call, re-commit yourself to it. Rejoice in your calling, accept that Jesus can take care of your limitations.

3.3 Personal: Our personal relationship with Jesus is about allowing him to come close without allowing ourselves to be scared off. Luke delights in showing how Simon came to commit himself to Jesus and become the leader of the apostles. The turning point is Jesus personal approach to him: 'May I use your boat?' Simon can readily agree to this. But it does not stop there. Jesus asks him to trust him in launching out again into the deep for a catch of fish. Simon has too much respect for him to say no, even if the experienced fisherman in him knows there is more chance of a catch in dusk or darkness than in broad sunshine. He is stunned by the catch, and reacts in a strange way (perhaps more appropriate to his post-resurrection re-call after his denial). In Luke's thinking he has reacted for you and me. How close do I want to come to God or to Jesus? How close can I come without realising my own sinfulness, unworthiness? But that realisation is grace. We miss the grace if we run away and keep God at a distance. He invites us to come close. He can overcome our sinfulness. He provides the catch of fish, not us. He accepts us unconditionally. 'Do not be afraid.' Look at your own call, how it has developed: are you still just an interested observer, trying to stay on the outside, or willing to go a step further?

3.4 Challenge: What a challenge Jesus offers to Simon, James and John. They may feel unworthy and scared, but they leave everything and follow him (just when they had caught their biggest catch of fish!). How is Jesus challenging me now? Have I allowed barriers to arise between myself and God? Do I think that Jesus couldn't be calling someone like me, with all my false starts and backsliding, to come closer to him, or to be more involved in my church, or parish? What are my fears? Am I able to listen to Jesus saying to me, 'Do not be afraid'? I must be patient with myself. Fear of closeness is a very human thing; closeness to God appears to be demanding. Yet Jesus is gentle with us, wishes only our joy and our fulfilment. Is there any one thing I think I might be called to do at his time? Is there something keeping me from doing it?

4. RESPONSE

The response in prayer and action needs to be very personal. Thank God for sending his Son, thank Jesus for his personal interest in each one of us, for his call and his patience with our response. Thank God for all those who have responded generously, and whose generosity has influenced us. Tell our fears honestly and ask for help to overcome them. Rest in his reassurance of us. Cast off the mooring ropes if you can, out into the deep water with Jesus. Remember that when he got Peter into deep water he took him by the hand. Make a renewed commitment to what you have been doing and decide to keep going and to do it gladly. We can begin things in excitement and joy, and feel richly blessed (God's abundance reflected in the free catch of fish). But we know that we can grow weary and let ourselves go through the motions with little heart. In the words of Mitch Albom, we can initially feel drenched by joy, then come to a dryness that requires root-tending (he applies it to marriage, but it is applicable to other vocations). 'Love, like joy, can nourish from above, drenching couples in soaking joy. But sometimes, under the angry heat of life, love grows dry on the surface, and must look to its roots, keeping itself alive.' (*The Five People You Meet in Heaven*, Time Warner Paperbacks, 2004, p 174)

Lord Jesus, I thank you for your acceptance of me, for the commitment I have been able to make already with your help. Help me to grow closer to you without fear, to try to walk where you lead me. Please do not give up on me when I stumble and falter. The love that we have wasted, O God of love, renew!

5. CONTEMPLATION

Try to practise the ancient piety of awareness of the presence of God, of Father, Son and Holy Spirit living within you, befriending you, delighting in your closeness to them. Walk with confidence in God's presence. Choose a text to live with, perhaps, following the late Pope John Paul II's challenge for the 21st century, 'Put out into the deep', and along with it, 'Do not be afraid'.

Prayer (repeated from the beginning):

Jesus, we thank you for calling us to be your disciples. We praise you with Mary, Zechariah and Simeon for all your blessings. Give us the grace to meet you personally, take away our fears. Help us to respond to your personal call to us. Help us to be humble in your presence, but to know that we are accepted, healed and loved. With this assurance, give us the courage to allow you to use us in your service. Amen.

Session 7: The Grateful Woman (Luke 7:36-50)
(Women disciples, 8:1-3)

1. FOCUS
Take time to focus the mind and heart, individually or in a group. For suggestions see Introduction p 18 or Session 1 p 26.

Prayer:
> Lord Jesus, when we are feeling low and ashamed of our own weakness, we lose heart. When we are doing well according to our own lights, we get self-righteous and lack compassion for others. Open our minds and hearts as we listen to your words when a righteous man meets a woman with a dark past in your presence. Help us to learn, from you, compassion and graciousness, and recognise the hope-filled future that you offer to all of us. Help us to see the goodness and potential in ourselves and others, and keep us from being chained by the past. Amen.

2. FAMILIARISATION
Read the story until you become familiar with the sequence of events and the people involved. Jesus is the central figure, the others react to him. The woman disrupts a grand social occasion, but Jesus is gracious to her, and challenging to the others.

Know them by their company!
> 7:36. One of the Pharisees asked Jesus to eat with him,
> and he went into the Pharisee's house
> and took his place at the table.
> 37. And a woman in the city, who was a sinner,
> having learned that he was eating in the Pharisee's house,
> brought an alabaster jar of ointment.
> 38. She stood behind him at his feet, weeping,
> and began to bathe his feet with her tears
> and to dry them with her hair.
> Then she continued kissing his feet
> and anointing them with the ointment.
> 39. Now when the Pharisee who had invited him saw it,
> he said to himself, 'If this man were a prophet,

he would have known who and what kind of woman this is
who is touching him – that she is a sinner.'

Forgiveness and love

40. Jesus spoke up and said to him,
'Simon, I have something to say to you.'
'Teacher,' he replied, 'Speak.'
41. 'A certain creditor had two debtors;
one owed five hundred denarii, and the other fifty.
42. When they could not pay,
he cancelled the debts for both of them.
Now which of then will love him more?'
43. Simon answered,
'I suppose the one for whom he cancelled the greater debt.'
And Jesus said to him, 'You have judged rightly.'
44. Then turning to the woman, he said to Simon,
'Do you see this woman? I entered your house;
you gave me no water for my feet,
but she has bathed my feet with her tears
and dried them with her hair.
45. You gave me no kiss, but from the time I came in
she has not stopped kissing my feet.
46. You did not anoint my head with ointment,
but she has anointed my feet with ointment.
47. Therefore, I tell you, her sins, which were many,
have been forgiven; hence she has shown great love.
But the one to whom little is forgiven, loves little.'
48. Then he said to her, 'Your sins are forgiven.'
49. But those who were at table with him began to say among
themselves, 'Who is this who even forgives sins?'
50. And he said to the woman,
'Your faith has saved you; go in peace.'

[Women disciples

8:1. Soon afterwards he went on through cities and villages,
proclaiming and bringing the good news of the kingdom of
God. The twelve were with him,
2. as well as some women
who had been cured of evil spirits and infirmities;
Mary, called Magdalene,

from whom seven demons had gone out,
3. and Joanna, the wife of Herod's steward Chuza,
and Susanna, and many others,
who provided for them out of their resources.]

2.1 Background

It is important for group leaders to be familiar with the background before leading a session. Others are encouraged to read the text and the background material before coming to a group session.

2.1.1 *Salvation* is one of the great themes of Luke's gospel. See, for example, 'To you is born this day in the city of David a saviour (2:11)', 'The Son of Man has come to seek out and save the lost (19:10).' Gratitude for the blessing of salvation is expressed in canticles by Mary, Zechariah, and Simeon. In this episode the woman pours out her love and gratitude in tangible gestures, without words. Jesus says to her, 'Your faith has saved you; go in peace' (v 50).

2.1.2 *At table with Jesus:* This is a simple story in one way: a woman with a shady past and a heady purpose appears to gate-crash an invitation dinner, in the house of a well-meaning but slightly self-righteous Pharisee, who wouldn't be seen dead in her presence. Jesus has received a polite, but not very warm welcome, lacking the usual courtesies for an important guest. The woman lavishes extravagant courtesies upon Jesus, who declares that this love shows she has been forgiven her sins, and is able to go in peace, assured of salvation. She alone touches the deeper meaning of what the scholars call 'table fellowship with Jesus', an invitation to hear God's message of acceptance and forgiveness and to receive the blessings of salvation.

2.1.3 *Forgiveness and gratitude:* The logic of the story is not quite so easy to follow, because of the ambiguity of the Greek words used in key places. It is possible to translate the Greek so that the woman displays great love and is therefore forgiven by Jesus. It is also possible, and fits better with the logic of the parable of the debtors used by Jesus, to translate in such a way that the woman has been already forgiven, and her gestures of love show her gratitude for that forgiveness. I follow this second line of interpretation. (For details see Fitzmeyer, Vol 1, pp 684-688) Thus

NRSV translates v 47, 'Therefore ... her sins, her many sins, have been forgiven; hence [Greek *hoti* could also be translated 'because'] she has shown such great love' (i.e., we can see that she must have been forgiven many sins, because she has been demonstrating such great love). Therefore, later, when Jesus says in v 48, 'Your sins are forgiven', he is giving a reassurance, a declaration of what has already happened. The other guests do ask the question, 'Who is this who even forgives sins?' That only serves for Luke to show that they ask the questions but do not really seek the answers, and to direct the reader, our Theophilus, and ourselves, to the realisation that it is through Jesus that God is offering forgiveness and salvation to the world.

2.1.4 Who is this woman? She is not named by Luke. There are, of course, no grounds for identifying her with Mary Magdalene (mentioned soon after in 8:2). This woman was known as a sinner, probably a prostitute; Mary Magdalene was freed from seven demons by Jesus (possibly from a mental illness), and there is no reason to think she was a prostitute. Luke shows delicacy in not naming the lady, if indeed any name was handed down, and Jesus mentions her many sins only to point up the abundance of her repentant love.

2.1.5 How did she get into a Pharisee's house? The scenario normally painted is that guests normally reclined at table before an open courtyard, where the devout and the curious could gather to hear edifying conversation. That would explain how the woman stands at the feet of Jesus.

2.1.6 Luke sets up a contrast between the play-safe Pharisee, Simon, and the passionate behaviour of the woman. Jesus gently suggests in the parable of the debtors that Simon is the 'little lover', and the woman is the 'great lover'. Simon is interested enough in hearing this new teacher, but certainly not committed to him. The woman has no eyes for anyone else but Jesus, and is commended for her faith. In Luke's stories of Jesus, there is usually one person who makes this commitment, while others miss the moment of grace, and it is very often the unexpected one, the outcast or the sinner who finds salvation. This is part of Luke's portrait of Jesus, concerned for the poor and the outcast. These stories bring hope to every A N Other who is lacking recognition, is belittled or abused, weak or foolish. Come to Jesus with confidence and find a gracious welcome, and a hope-filled future.

2.1.7 Jesus' graciousness: this woman would 'affront you' if you were trying to keep up appearances of respectability. But Jesus is not embarrassed, and treats the lady disciple graciously. He accepts her ministrations, the tears, the foot-washing and the anointing, and defends her in the presence of Simon, who sees only her past, not her repentance or her new relationship with Jesus.

3. REFLECTION
After a period of quiet reflection on the text, the group leader may wish to ask individuals to share briefly on what has struck them most forcefully in the passage.

3.1 Journey: This story is about the inner journey of the woman from a place of darkness to inner peace, salvation, and a close relationship with Jesus. We are all on that journey, so we wish to learn all we can about it here. As we will see in the Prodigal Son story (session 13), the moment of grace is his coming to his senses and the decision to return to his father. In this case it is the decision of the woman to buy the jar of ointment and to find Jesus, to show that she has heard his teaching and comes in repentance (we cannot rule out a previous meeting with Jesus, but we have no evidence for it). The returning son plans a speech and rationalises it; the woman brings ointment, weeps and washes Jesus' feet, communicating her feelings in gestures without words. She does not hide her past, cares not for the reactions of the onlookers, weeps tears of sorrow and joy, for she has already had great burdens lifted from her soul. She is now filled with gratitude, which she is determined to demonstrate, no matter who sees it. Gratitude for perceived blessings is the beginning of religion, of every close relationship to God, the stuff of a eucharistic consciousness, the inspiration to praise and worship. Note how the woman unselfconsciously focuses on the person of Jesus, and his gracious acceptance of her ministrations. Reflect: do you remember this experience of being forgiven, of the return of joy and the need to express it in love? Have you experienced this gracious welcome from Jesus? Would you like to? Imagine yourself anointing the feet of Jesus. Imagine yourself on this inner journey with the woman, from emptiness to a heart bursting with love and gratitude. Imagine Jesus receiving you graciously. Be sure Jesus will say to many of us: you *have* done this for me. Because you have done it for one of my brothers and sisters.

3.2 Joy: This episode is the expression in action of the same gratitude for God's blessings that we find expressed in the canticles of the early chapters. This is a theme dear to Luke, that the disciple of Jesus should be very conscious of being richly blessed, and should sing those blessings, using words if necessary. This woman's actions speak louder than words. Reflect: do we ever come into the presence of the Lord in prayer or in church with a focus like this woman's on the person of Jesus? Think of how we often enter a church casually, greet our neighbour instead of the Lord, look to see who else is there and how they are dressed. Take a moment now to re-focus on Jesus, and express our thanks and joy that he has called us into his presence. 'Lift up your hearts … it is right to give him thanks and praise.'

3.2 Personal: Look at the relationships in the story. A tentative relationship between Simon the host and Jesus, a barrier between Simon and the sinful woman, who is in fact a forgiven woman, a strong and growing relationship between the woman and Jesus, confirmed by his words, 'Your sins have been forgiven … your faith has saved you; go in peace.' This woman does us this great service: she shows that what is most important for each of us is our relationship with Jesus and our experience of his forgiveness and loving acceptance. Reflect: what do I need to do to be closer to him? Does this story renew my faith in his welcoming love? Do I allow past sins, failures, hurts to be obstacles to my trust in his welcome? Have I difficulty in forgiving myself, and so don't feel worthy of being accepted? Does past experience of stern authority figures make it difficult for me to trust Jesus? Do I see people's past like Simon, and not their potential, their future, like Jesus? Am I satisfied with a superficial relationship with Jesus like that of Simon?

3.3 Challenge: This episode challenges us to reflect on our experience of forgiveness, or lack of it, and our experience of forgiving, or not forgiving. Some carry a burden of guilt with them for years: it is time to lay down the burden at the feet of Jesus, and experience his graciousness. Time to go to the sacrament of reconciliation if necessary and take responsibility for what we have done and find forgiveness, or sometimes to find what we have considered guilt was misinformation or misguided advice in the past. 'Come to me, all who are heavily burdened, and I will give you rest.' Time to demonstrate our gratitude in action, perhaps. Time to see good in people rather than their past failures. Time to remember to keep alive with prayer our close relationship with Jesus. Formulate a few resolutions that might help you to be more responsive to Jesus and his people.

4. RESPONSE

A personal response of thanksgiving is important. We give thanks to the Lord for the forgiveness and healing we have received. We ask for the courage to seek it when we need to. We ask for trust in God's goodness, and we ask the Lord to help us to believe in our own goodness – a received goodness, but a lovely gift to be used. Ask for the gift of joy: if we do not have it, we can be sure that Jesus wishes to give it. 'I have said these things to you so that my joy may be in you, and that your joy may be complete' (John 15:11). Unite ourselves with Jesus in the Eucharist, as he gives himself into the hands of God his Father for us; unite ourselves to our people giving thanks to God every day and everywhere through the Eucharist. Ask for help to forgive those who may have hurt us, ask for help to see the good in them. 'Blessed be the Lord God of Israel, for he has looked favourably on his people and redeemed them. He has raised up a mighty saviour for us in the house of his servant David' (1:68f).

5. CONTEMPLATION

Keep the attitude of thankfulness and joy which we have found, through living with this gospel story, in our hearts and minds. Try to look with love and acceptance upon others, knowing how Jesus loves them. Choose a text to remind you of the story and turn it over in your mind: e.g. 'Your faith has saved you, go in peace', or 'Your sins have been forgiven', or 'The one to whom little is forgiven, loves little.'

Prayer:

Lord Jesus, we bless and praise you for the healing and forgiveness that you bring to us. Increase our faith in your forgiving love, and help us to be grateful for that love. Thank
you for wanting to be close to us, for wishing to live in our
hearts. Help us always to be close to you, and grant us the
grace to forgive others as we have been ourselves forgiven.
Amen.

May steadfast faith sustain us,
And hope made firm in you,
The love that we have wasted,
O God of love, renew.
(From the Breviary, Vol III, Morning Prayer, Tuesday, week 3)

Session 8: Who do you say that I am? (Luke 9:18-27)

1. FOCUS
Take time to focus the mind and heart. For suggestions, see Introduction p 18, or Session 1 p 26.

Prayer:
> Lord Jesus, you ask each one of us, 'Who do you say I am?' Help us by your grace and the gifts of your Spirit to know you better. Give us the grace to praise you in times of joy, and the courage to follow you in times of sorrow and pain. Teach us through your word the meaning of being a disciple, and the joy of walking in your footsteps. Amen

2. FAMILIARISATION
Read the text below a few times, until you are familiar with it. There are three parts: (1) Jesus' questions and Peter's response of faith, (2) Jesus' first prophecy of his passion, and (3) Jesus' words addressed to all about the implications of discipleship. Close your eyes and get the sequence of events/ideas clear, even if not the details.

Peter's profession of faith in the Messiah
> 9:18 Once when Jesus was praying alone,
> with only the disciples near him,
> he asked them, 'Who do the crowds say I am?'
> 19 They answered, 'John the Baptist, but others, Elijah;
> and others still, that one of the ancient prophets has arisen.'
> 20 He said to them, 'But who do you say that I am?'
> Peter answered, 'The Messiah [Christ] of God.'

The coming passion and resurrection
> 21 He sternly ordered and commanded them
> not to tell anyone,
> 22 saying, 'The Son of Man must undergo great suffering,
> and be rejected by the elders, chief priests and scribes,
> and be killed,
> and on the third day be raised.'

All disciples must share in Jesus' destiny
   23 Then he said to them all, [*pros pantas*, 'to everyone']
  'If any want to become my followers,
  let them deny themselves
  and take up their cross daily and follow me.
   24 For those who want to save their life will lose it,
  and those who lose their life for my sake will save it.
   25 What does it profit them if they gain the whole world,
  and lose or forfeit themselves?
   26 Those who are ashamed of me and of my words,
  of them the Son of Man will be ashamed
  when he comes in his glory
  and the glory of the Father and of the holy angels.
   27 But truly I tell you, there are some standing here
  who will not taste death
  before they have seen the kingdom of God.

2.1 Background
Please try to read the background notes in advance of the group session. Group leaders especially need to have a grasp of this material before leading a session. Read the text again in the light of this background before going to the Reflection stage.

2.1.1 The question to be answered: From 9:9 Luke has been giving answers to the question posed by Herod the Tetrarch (Herod Antipas, whom the Romans allowed to govern Galilee): 'John I beheaded, but who is this about whom I hear such talk?' Herod is typical of those who are curious, but not in any way committed to Jesus. Only those who watch and pray, and wish to become disciples, reach proper answers. Luke's first (implicit) answer comes in the miracle of the loaves and fishes, immediately before our passage (9:10-17), although there, unusually for Luke, no reaction of the crowd is given. That is now followed by Peter's declaration that Jesus is the Messiah (9:20). Jesus' questions have prompted the disciples to give firstly the tentative answers given by the crowds, and the much better (though still incomplete) answer of Peter, representing the faith of the disciples: 'The Messiah of God.'

2.1.2 Luke's sequence: Luke follows the sequence of Mark, but gives it a different slant, chiefly by what he omits. In the parallel passage in Mark (8:27–9:1), Peter reacts with incredulity to Jesus' prophecy of the passion and is soundly rebuked by Jesus. Matthew (16:13-28) allows Peter to make a more complete confession of faith, followed by Jesus' words about the church and the power of the keys given to Peter, before reverting to Mark's sequence. Luke 'streamlines' the passage, omitting any reference to misunderstanding by Peter or any other disciple. This is in line with Luke's great reverence for the disciples and especially Peter. They are the intimate friends of Jesus, and he omits their failures where possible. But Luke gives us a rich and very powerful sequence for our reflection: the confession of faith by Peter, the prophecy of the passion (and resurrection, though this is not comprehended by the disciples), and the declaration to everyone (not just the Twelve) that loyal followers of Jesus would have to share in his destiny.

2.1.3 What kind of Messiah? Jesus gives very strict orders not to tell anyone he is Messiah, and immediately begins to speak of his suffering, rejection and death. Jewish expectation, shared by the disciples, was for a royal Messiah to restore the line of David, and any thought of the failure or rejection of such a divinely sent figure was totally alien to their picture of the Messiah. They never dreamt he would be the Son of God in the strict sense, the Eternal Son Incarnate. They did not yet know about the doctrine of the Trinity. That would be revealed only after their experience of Jesus' resurrection and the coming of the Spirit at Pentecost. But they expected the Messiah to be a powerful figure, who would quickly sort out the oppressors of God's people (including the Romans), and the sinners. There is no need to go too far and say that the Jews expected a Messiah with a totally political agenda, without religious implications. But there was enough royal messianic fervour to make Jesus very reluctant to accept the title of Messiah, without qualifying it with the prophecy of suffering and coming rejection. In the Baptism of Jesus (session 4), we saw that Jesus' mission is to be Servant-Messiah. Our present passage represents a steep learning curve for the disciples. Luke will expand the narrative of Jesus' journey to Jerusalem (see session 10), so that on the journey disciples may be instructed, and prepared, as far as they were able to comprehend, for the great events to come in Jerusalem.

2.1.4 Sharing the Master's destiny: By addressing Jesus' words about following him 'to everyone' (v 23), not just to the Twelve, and adding the phrase 'daily' to 'take up their cross', Luke makes it clear that Jesus' words about following him apply to all disciples everywhere, and therefore to us. This can be a hard lesson for us, too. The importance of learning this lesson cannot be over-emphasised; it is the central wisdom of the gospel. It is not just that in order to follow Jesus we must accept the daily 'crosses' that come our way and carry them with courage, though that is good. It is that this following of Jesus' unselfish love and giving of himself should become our way of life, our mind-set. Life comes out of giving, sacrificing, dying. Our little daily dyings are our way to find the fullness of life. Unwillingness to follow this way of Jesus, our daily selfishness, is destructive of our true life: 'for those who want to save their life will lose it' (v 24). Jesus is patient with the Twelve while they learn the lesson, and he will be patient with us.

3. REFLECTION
Take time to reflect quietly on the text. Did you notice that Jesus was praying as the scene opened? Play the scene over in your mind. The leader of a group may wish to ask volunteers to share briefly what initially strikes them about the passage.

3.1 Journey: There is no physical journey, yet the reader is given a panorama of the whole drama of salvation, Jesus' identity, his suffering, his death, his being raised up, his future coming in glory, and the promise that disciples will experience the power of the coming of the kingdom before they die. For the disciples, it maps out a difficult journey they will have to undertake to be with Jesus. It is a journey through death to life, for Jesus and for disciples. We need the guidance of the Holy Spirit to help us on our journey of understanding. As I grow older, and find that I have to give up things I used to relish, I perhaps begin to understand better that losing my life will find it, saving my life will lose it. It is not a question of martyrdom, in the real or figurative sense, but the clearer realisation that I must follow Jesus through death to new life, and that there is no other way. So I need to choose that as my lifestyle, and rejoice that at last I may get it right! Following Jesus means less selfishness, accepting the limitations of my humanity gracefully, more giving, to and for others. Daily! Daily sacrifices mean little deaths, but little resurrections also. Finding life, life that endures and is the real me. Jesus says, gain the world and lose yourself.

3.2 Joy: Where is the joy here? Jesus seems to paint a grim picture. I fear that if I enter fully into this discipleship, it will be the great kill-joy. Austerity reigns? Yet the saints are not sad. St Teresa of Avila prayed, 'From sour-faced saints, O Lord, deliver us.' The Christian conviction is that if Jesus asks us to do hard things, it is always in love, and for our good. His dearest wish is that we become truly ourselves and find life. 'Those that lose their life for my sake will find it' – not just in heaven, but in the daily resurrections of everyday life. We are still tinged with the old fear that this is a valley of tears, and there will only be joy in the life to come. But being true to myself, and to my deepest convictions, gives deep joy, already here. Maybe it is not what the world calls 'happiness'. It is not the pleasure of the moment, but more lasting, truer, deep down joy. This is so even when things go wrong, and there is sorrow in life. I am following him, and he is with me. I am doing it for his sake, in love. That is the source of joy.

3.3 Personal: These words have deep personal meaning for Jesus, for the first disciples and, as Luke says, 'for everyone'. Jesus reveals his whole life and destiny. It is about who he is. We can only surmise the many hours of prayer and reflection he has devoted to his coming ordeal; he was at prayer as this episode began. He is called Messiah, but that title is too ambiguous, so he adds 'Son of Man', which points to glory earned the hard way, through facing suffering and opposition.

Luke, unlike Mark and Matthew, does not dwell on the reactions of the disciples at this point. Yet Jesus' destiny is revealed to them with devastating realism, and it is not what they dreamed of. They will only gradually comprehend the shattering revelation, after they have plumbed the depths of their human weakness in the passion and death of Jesus. For now they must live with questions, which is what human beings must do in the face of the mystery of suffering – follow the Lord until the answers begin to make some sense.

For us, who are able to look at the plan of salvation, laid out before our eyes, from the perspective of 2000 years, it is still difficult to embrace with love and acceptance. We become conscious of our weakness, our love of comfort and possessions and of our own way. But each is called to answer the question, 'Who is this Jesus?' Will I follow a suffering Messiah? Will I try to be faithful no matter what happens? Will I never be ashamed of him? Never disown him? I know I have been weak in the past. Will that prevent me from making a new commitment? Is my personal prayer strong enough to sustain me? Is my personal relationship with Jesus strong enough? 'If any want to become my followers …' I need to 'want to', to have a strong desire to follow Jesus.

3.4 Challenge: Yes! It is not difficult to see how this applies. Jesus is conscious of what his own challenge is, and he gives the example of courage and determination. He calls disciples then and now to follow him with courage. He makes clear, in that paradoxical way, what is the road to finding one's real self, integrity, salvation and life. For many people the daily cross is very real, because of illness, broken relationships, the need to give up what they used to be able to do, as age and infirmity take away freedoms. Sometimes the challenge is to speak out about our faith, sometimes to put it into practice. The need to pray about this is clear.

4. RESPONSE

Our response must be personal. Express as you can faith in Jesus, and in his way of doing things. Express gratitude to him for taking this journey for us, and for thinking that we are worth involving in the process. Express hope: hope means that I can see the goal and know how to get there with divine help. Express confidence that that help will always be given, that nothing else is better or more life-giving for me that following Jesus. Ask for the love to commit oneself to Jesus. Thank God for every experience we have had of his love, compassion, forgiveness, and sustaining care. These experiences teach me that God is faithful. Jesus was patient with the disciples when they failed; he will be patient with us too. Ask forgiveness for failing in the past; believe that it is given freely. Beg the Father to strengthen our commitment to Jesus. Ask the Holy Spirit for guidance, for help to make good choices, and to follow them through. There may be something that I need courage to do at this time; pray for it. Sometimes I just need to keep going. Ask the Lord to support those whose daily sacrifices are very real, that they may be given courage and endurance.

5. CONTEMPLATION

Keep this passage in mind as you go about your daily routines. Try to let it influence the choices you make, the kindness you show to others, the warmth of your relationships. Choose a text to live with: 'Those who want to save their life will lose it', or 'Let them deny themselves and take up their cross daily and follow me.'

Prayer:

Father, through your great love and the gifts of the Holy Spirit, teach us to understand the meaning of your Son's death and resurrection, and help us to reflect it in our lives. We ask this through Christ our Lord. Amen.

Session 9: The Transfiguration (Luke 9:28-36)

1. FOCUS

Take time to focus the mind and heart on the presence of the Lord. For suggestions see Introduction p 18, or Session 1 p 26.

Prayer:

God our Father, your Son, the Chosen One, came to you in prayer, filled with awareness of his coming destiny in Jerusalem, knowing how shocking the news was to his disciples. You drew Jesus' humanity to yourself until his inner being shone with light. You allowed the disciples to see his glory, and you spoke to them from heaven. Lord, we rejoice in your Son's glory in heaven, and we wish to follow him and to know him better. We bring to you our fears and worries. Help us to see the greatness of your beloved Son, and to listen to his voice. Let the light of his glory shine on our sick and those who are troubled in spirit, so that we may all feast on the power that comes from his passion, death and resurrection. Amen.

2. FAMILIARISATION

Read (or listen to) the text a few times to become familiar with it. Close your eyes and go over the sequence of events in your mind.

Introduction
>   9:28 Now about eight days after these sayings,
>   Jesus took with him Peter and John and James,
>   and went up on the mountain to pray.

Wonder to behold
>   29 And while he was praying,
>   the appearance of his face changed,
>   and his clothes became dazzling white.
>   30 Suddenly they saw two men,
>   Moses and Elijah, talking to him.
>   *[lit. and behold, two men were talking to him, who were M and E]*
>   31 They appeared in glory
>   and were speaking of his departure *[exodus]*, cf 9:51
>   which he was about to accomplish *[fulfil]* at Jerusalem.

The disciples see the vision, with limited understanding

    32 Now Peter and his companions
    were weighed down with sleep;
    but since they had stayed awake,
    [*startled into full wakefulness?*]
    they saw his glory and the two men who stood with him.
    33 Just as they were leaving him, Peter said to Jesus,
    'Master, it is good for us to be here;
    let us make three dwellings,
    one for you, one for Moses and one for Elijah'
    – not knowing what he said.

A voice from heaven

    34 While he was saying this,
    a cloud came and overshadowed them;
    and they were terrified as they entered the cloud.
    35 Then from the cloud came a voice that said,
    'This is my Son, my Chosen; listen to him!' (Is 42:1; Lk 3:22;
    Mt 3:17)

Conclusion

    36 When the voice had spoken, Jesus was found alone.
    And they kept silent and in those days told no one
    any of the things they had seen.

2. 1 Background

Group leaders should become familiar with the background material before leading a session. Participants in a group session are encouraged to read the text and the Background before the session begins.

2.1.1 The Context. The episode comes immediately after the first prophecy of the passion and resurrection, and the words of Jesus to the disciples about sharing in his destiny, carrying the cross after him (9:21-27). Though no words of reaction come from the disciples in Luke, not even from Peter, it is to be presumed that they were in some state of shock. At 9:44 we have a second prophecy of the passion. At 9:51 we have the beginning of the journey narrative; Jesus sets out for Jerusalem, the city of destiny, 'when the time drew near for him to be taken up' (Greek *analempsis*, lifting up, assumption).

2.1.2 Jesus goes up the mountain 'to pray' (frequent stress in Luke on Jesus' prayer). It is in prayer to the Father that this inner light shines forth. God's plan is twofold: to strengthen his Son's humanity for the coming ordeal and to strengthen the disciples, whose notion of what the Messiah is to be has been shattered by Jesus' words about betrayal and death. Therefore the words from heaven are addressed to the disciples: 'This is my Son … listen to him.' This theme of listening to Jesus will recur in the post-resurrection appearances, where Luke stresses that Jesus has to guide us to understand the scriptural references to the Messiah, so that we may understand the meaning of his death and resurrection.

2.1.3 Moses and Elijah appear with Jesus. They are usually said to represent the Law and the Prophets, both testifying to Jesus. In Luke they are seen 'in glory', both seen as 'assumed' into heaven. Moses died alone and his grave was never found (Deuteronomy 34); later there was popular speculation that he had been taken up like Elijah. Elijah's taking up in a chariot of fire is found in 2 Kings chapter 2. They both also had experience of the divine presence on Mount Sinai (Horeb). They are described as talking to Jesus about his *'exodus'* (lit. *journey out*), which he is to *'fulfil'* in Jerusalem. The *exodus* refers to Jesus' journey to the Father, his passion, death and resurrection (compare the 'taking up' in 9:51).

2.1.4 The disciples, though heavy with sleep, stay awake (perhaps 'are brought fully awake') and see Jesus' glory (*doxa*). That is sometimes seen as showing that this is really a resurrection story brought back into the public ministry, but this is unlikely. 'Glory' refers to Jesus' inner reality, his union with God, his mysterious being shining through. The term is also used of the second coming 'in glory', but never used in the resurrection appearances.

2.1.5 The cloud is a scriptural way of referring to the (hidden) presence of God (as in the exodus from Egypt). The voice from heaven is addressed to the disciples, and there may be an emphasis on 'listen to *him*' (i.e. take your understanding of what the Messiah is to be from Jesus, not from the prophets, or at least, from the prophets as Jesus interprets them for you).

3. REFLECTION

Take a period of quiet reflection on the text. What initially strikes you about the text? Group leaders may wish to ask volunteers to share initial impressions with the group.

3.1 Journey: Jesus goes up the mountain to pray. The mountain is the sacred place where we encounter God – the place of revelation, or of prayer. Where do we go to pray? It need not always be a physical place – we can travel within. Jesus is soon to begin his journey to Jerusalem, but the subject of the communication between Jesus and the prophets Moses and Elijah is his exodus, the journey to the Father. Disciples have to share in that journey to the Father, learning from Jesus on the way. The idea of exodus is a rich one: it applies to every bit of progress we make from a familiar but limited state to a freer, richer one, though perhaps one fraught with danger. Think of examples: learning to walk, learning a new skill, risking new friendship, getting married, and the biggest one, facing death. Jesus invites us to bring our fears to God in prayer, to find the Father's strengthening love surround us on our journey. 'Be not afraid, for I am with you.' Accompanying Jesus prayerfully on his journey (e.g., during Lent) helps us to face our own fears.

3.2 Joy: What sustains and nourishes us, gives our lives meaning and purpose, in this story? It must have been for Jesus himself a tremendously nurturing experience of the Father's loving presence, giving him courage and resolve. The apostles saw his glory, glimpsed the mysterious reality of Jesus' relationship to the Father, felt terrified when overshadowed by the cloud (awe in God's presence), were confirmed in their discipleship by the voice from heaven. If we represent Theophilus, to whom the gospel is addressed, our faith in Jesus, the Son of God, the Chosen One, is nourished. We share in his glory now through the sacraments; we will share in his glory for ever if we remain faithful. This requires trust: we may be on an exodus experience at this time, and be afraid, conscious of our fragility; or we may know people who are ill, even facing death. Jesus wants us to experience in prayer the supporting love of God our Father, who reveals to us his love and our own inner strength.

3.3 Personal: Jesus shares a deep experience with God the Father, with Moses and Elijah, with his chosen disciples. Peter, James and John have an experience of living in mystery, and meeting the divine, which will literally stand to them all their lives, even though they will be weak again. God invites us to come to him for healing, to trust in his Son, to share the glory of Jesus. God asks us to lose our fears, to find the gifts that are within us, and use them. Where am I afraid? What gifts am I not using? How do I handle disappointment, illness, loss? Where am I invited to go for strength? Do I answer the invitation or try to tackle everything on my own?

3.4 Challenge: God strengthens Jesus and the disciples, not by telling them it is not going to happen, but by helping them to see the end of the journey, the help God can give them, and their own inner strength. Life has many challenges for us, and this text brings us face to face with the reality of our own fragility, and the need to trust in Jesus, and in God our Father. Jesus faces up to his own death, calls disciples to share his destiny – both the dying and the rising to glory.

4. RESPONSE

Take time for personal response in prayer. Make acts of thanksgiving for the Father's watchful presence over Jesus, over the disciples, over us. Thank him for the courage of Jesus in facing his exodus. Thank God for our baptism, for our baptismal journey, which will end, not in death, but in life with the Father. Accept the place on that journey where each of us now finds ourselves. Pray for those who may be facing critical stages of their own journey, that they may be strengthened, and know that Jesus journeys with them. Give thanks for the glory of the Lord, in which we already share, and will share in full, if we are faithful. Resolve to carry our personal crosses with patience. Offer ourselves with Jesus in the Eucharist. Ask for a sense of trust in God our Father, who sees each of us as his beloved sons and daughters. Listen to the Beloved Son of God: what is he trying to say to us now?

5. CONTEMPLATION

Keep the mood of your prayer with you, as you go about your daily activities. Choose a favourite phrase or sentence to live with, let it resonate within you, e.g., 'This is my Son, my Chosen; listen to him.' Be in a listening mode, hearing the voice of Jesus, and the voices of others around you.

Prayer:
> *(from the Missal for the feast of the Transfiguration, 6 August)*
> God our Father, in the transfigured glory of Christ your Son,
> you strengthen our faith
> by confirming the witness of your prophets,
> and show us the splendour of your beloved sons and daughters.
> As we listen to the voice of your Son,
> help us to become heirs to eternal life with him,
> for he lives and reigns with you and the Holy Spirit,
> one God, for ever and ever, Amen

Session 10: Setting out for Jerusalem (Luke 9: 51-62)

1. FOCUS

Focus the mind and the heart on the presence of God. For suggestions see Introduction p 18, or Session 1 p 26.

Prayer:

Lord, as we listen to our friend St Luke telling us how you set out for Jerusalem with determination and courage, we wish to say that we desire to follow you wherever it takes us. But you know our hesitation, our weakness and our proneness to wander from the chosen path. So help us, Lord; give us your courage and determination, and guide us with your Holy Spirit. May we walk with you, knowing that you are always with us. Amen.

2. FAMILIARISATION

Read the text a few times with care, until you become familiar with it. Put yourself in the place of disciples following Jesus, and listen to what Jesus says about what it takes to follow him. Close your eyes and go over the stages of the story in your mind.

Decision to begin the journey
9:51 When the days drew near
for him to be taken up, [*lit. for his taking up, analempsis, a taking up*]
he set his face to go to Jerusalem.

Dealing with opposition
52 And he sent messengers ahead of him.
On their way they entered a village of the Samaritans
to make ready for him;
53 but they did not receive him,
because his face was set towards Jerusalem.
54 When his disciples, James and John, saw it, they said,
'Lord, do you want us to command fire
to come down from heaven and consume them?'
55 But he turned and rebuked them.
56 Then they went off to another village. [*alternative reading*:
… rebuked them, and said, you do not know what spirit you

94

are of, for the Son of Man has not come to destroy the lives of human beings, but to save them. Then …]

Discipleship and tough love
57 As they were going along the road, someone said to him.
'I will follow you wherever you go.'
58 And Jesus said to him,
'Foxes have holes, and birds of the air have nests;
but the Son of Man has nowhere to lay his head.'
59 And to another he said,
'Follow me.'
But he said, 'Lord, first let me go and bury my father.'
60 But Jesus said to him,
'Let the dead bury their own dead;
but as for you, go and proclaim the kingdom of God.'
61 Another said, 'I will follow you, Lord;
but first let me say farewell to those at my home.'
62 Jesus said to him,
'No one who puts his hand to the plough and looks back
is fit for the kingdom of God.'

2.1 Background
This material is given to help your understanding of the text. It should be read before the stage of Reflection, certainly by group leaders, and all participants in a group should endeavour to read the text and the Background notes before coming to a group session.

2.1.1 The Journey Narrative: This is the beginning of what is called Luke's 'journey narrative'. If you read ahead you will see various references to 'making his way to Jerusalem', but you will find Jesus entering Jerusalem at last in chapter 19, coming to the temple at 19:45. The exact geography of the journey is not easily followed, because for Luke it is a symbolic journey as well a physical one. It is a motif, a theological idea, Jesus the Saviour going to his destiny, Jesus the teacher training his disciples how to follow him. Disciples are by definition learners (from Latin *discere*, to learn), and Luke includes in this narrative a body of instructional material for disciples then and now. So on the way to Jerusalem, the disciples learn about the sacrifices involved in following Jesus, and they have to learn quite quickly.

Immediately after the decision to go to Jerusalem, they encounter the first opposition to Jesus in a Samaritan village, and learn that Jesus' way of dealing with it is different from theirs. Then Luke has included three sayings of Jesus about discipleship, demanding statements that call for total commitment. The journey will be a tough training school for the disciples, preparing them for the crisis to come. The question remains, will they be ready when they are put to the test?

2.1.2 Man of Decision: Though Luke presents Jesus as compassionate, good company, welcoming sinners and outcasts, it would be a mistake to think that Jesus in Luke is undemanding or wishy-washy. Jesus is here presented as a man of decision, looking his destiny squarely in the eye, setting off to meet it, ready to face any opposition, not with violence, but with steadfast fidelity to the plan of God. Disciples who follow him are expected to be fully committed, ready to share in his destiny, following him on his exodus journey to Jerusalem, and to the Father. As we read Luke's words and try to learn, we are also disciples following Jesus to – no, *through* – death, and to the Father. This journey symbolises our baptismal journey, an exodus we all have to complete. 'I have decided to write ... most excellent Theophilus, so that you may know the truth'(1:3-4).

2.1.3 Samaria: Luke is the only gospel, other than John, which tells of Jesus' dealing with Samaritans. Samaria was the region between Judea and Galilee, the remnant of the old Northern Kingdom, most of whose people had been transported into exile by the Assyrians, and replaced by Gentiles who intermarried with the Israelites. Though they believed in God and accepted the Pentateuch, the Jews looked upon them with hostility, for historical reasons, and they had to build themselves a temple on Mt Gerizim, near modern Nablus, on the West Bank, where a small number of Samaritans still survive. In Acts chapter 8, Luke describes the conversion of many Samaritans, and the sending of Peter and John 'that they might receive the Holy Spirit' (8:15) – John was one of those who wanted to call down fire on them, as Elijah did (2 Kings 1:9-12). Following Jesus' way will bring salvation to Samaritans and Gentiles.

2.1.4 The Hard Sayings: Luke puts together three sayings of Jesus to represent the call to leave everything and follow Jesus, and the urgency of the decision. Not everyone is called to leave home, but those who are called are called to total commitment. The first would-be disciple (vv 57-58) is an enthusiast who has not thought out the implications of following a teacher on the road, with no fixed abode. Jesus is looking for a serious commitment, people who will last the pace. The second and third represent commitment that is provisional or postponed. They give family reasons (prior commitments). 'To bury my father' seems a very compelling reason, and Jesus' reply seems harsh. But probably the father is aging, not yet dead, and the man wants to stay at home while his father is still alive; after he dies he will of course become a disciple. Jesus hard words, 'Let the dead bury their own dead', have a spiritual meaning: let the spiritually dead, those who do not respond to the call, stay at home and bury the dead. The spiritually alive have the duty to proclaim the kingdom of God. The third candidate reminds us of the call of Elisha in 1 Kings 19:19-21; he also wanted to say goodbye to his family, but realised the urgency of the call, burned his plough and sacrificed his oxen, and followed Elijah. Jesus calls for commitment that does not admit of looking backwards.

3. REFLECTION
After a few moments of quiet reflection, the group leader may wish to ask volunteers to share briefly their initial reaction to the passage.

3.1 Journey: Jesus' journey and the call to discipleship are the twin themes of this passage. Jesus sets out with determination, yet with peace in his heart. Opposition will not stop him, but he will not look for confrontation, nor offer violence to save himself. His journey is not just to the cross, but through the cross to the Father in the resurrection. The disciples are less sure about everything: about the suffering to come, about what they should do about opposition, about peaceful means to save themselves, about the end of the journey, about the elusive concept of Jesus rising again. So the journey is going to be a difficult learning experience. We are on our baptismal journey, following Jesus through death to the Father in the resurrection. That is our faith statement. In fact, we are learners (disciples), coming to terms with the realities, just like the disciples: with the difficulties of the journey, with opposition, with non-violence, with our inevitable death, with the reality of the resurrection, with unconditional loyalty to Jesus. None of this is easy for us. Jesus did not find it easy either: does that console us? He has sought his clarity and determination in deep prayer to the Father, and in the Father's affirmation of his decisions, as we saw in the Transfiguration (Session 9). Jesus is trying to draw us into that habit of prayer to God our Father. Therefore chapter 11 is full of Jesus teaching on prayer. The disciples sense where Jesus gets his strength, and ask: 'Lord, teach us to pray'(11:1). They are to pray to the Father, 'do not bring us to the time of trial' [lead us not into temptation] (11:4), and be confident that God our Father will give the Holy Spirit to those who ask him (11:13).

3.2 *Joy:* There's no obvious joy in this passage. Yet if that is so, then the basic truths of the Christian faith bring us no joy. That cannot be true. So look again. God's plan for our salvation has been announced. The consequences are now becoming clearer. The full meaning of it is not yet understood by the disciples, why Jesus faces death, the meaning of the resurrection, the full life he promises to those who imitate his sacrifice. But we know the whole story, looking back with hindsight. So we know that Jesus is teaching us how to overcome sin and suffering, how to turn it into joy and life; we know the wonder of the resurrection, and our sharing in the new life of the risen Christ. We are following Jesus now full of that new life, full of the gifts of the Holy Spirit. The basic Christian call to discipleship is joy-full, but with a joy that does not deny reality, rather accepts it and fills it with the love of Jesus. We are speaking here of deep joy and the knowledge that we are truly held in God's love, even in the midst of suffering. Jesus shows tough love, but real love, in calling us to live authentic lives of unselfishness and self-giving love. The well-known poster says, 'Lord, I expect nothing to happen this day, which you and I cannot handle together.'

3.3 *Personal:* What speaks to the core of our being has to be personal. We see Jesus' personal faith in his Father's call and his courage in facing what is to come. He teaches the disciples to realise what kind of Messiah they are following. James and John, the fiery ones, begin to learn another way. Jesus is giving that message to us also. Approach others peacefully: if one way is blocked, try another one. Perhaps we identify with one or other of the would-be disciples whom Jesus challenges: the thoughtless enthusiast who will not last the course, or the procrastinator who is going to do big things some day, but not today, thank you. Jesus is personally calling us to more realism in our discipleship.

3.4 Challenge: Few passages are more challenging. Few bring out the Lucan portrait of Jesus better. The following of Jesus is demanding, and in Luke's understanding, the disciple is expected to be totally committed. The disciples then were certainly challenged. So are we. How deep is my personal attachment to Jesus, and to his way of doing things? What do I need to change in my life? Do I expect the following of Jesus to protect me from all sorrow, conflict and distress? Do I feel let down when sickness or sorrow comes to my doorstep? We hear words like this: 'I've always gone to Mass and said my prayers. Why is God letting this happen to me?' Obviously Jesus does not think his disciples will be immune from suffering. Our mind tells us that is true, but it is harder to overcome our feelings. It is all right to be in touch with our feelings, and harmful to deny them. But our choices must be based on reality and truth, not only on our feelings. Admit your feelings, and know the Lord understands. But he loves you enough to challenge you.

4. RESPONSE

Rejoice in being a disciple of Jesus. Rejoice in his strength, his carrying of our burdens. Pray for help to be like Jesus: decisive, courageous, peaceful. *Lord, help us to stand up for our beliefs, but to treat others who may differ from us with love and acceptance. Help us not to put off important choices, not to be eternal procrastinators. Lord, sustain us in our weakness when we face hard decisions; help us to admit our weakness, but to rely on your strength. Help us to know that we can grow through sacrifice. Help us to love unselfishly. Help us to learn from your giving of yourself into the hands of God. Help us to be close to you, Lord, in the Eucharist, to unite ourselves with your offering. Forgive us our failures and help us to accept our human limitations, and forgive ourselves. Give us a longing for your gift of life, for the presence of the Holy Spirit, who gives strength to our human weakness.*

5. CONTEMPLATION

Keep our eyes on Jesus. Remember what we do when we make the sign of the cross upon ourselves. At the beginning of the gospel at Mass, we have the custom of putting the cross on our forehead, lips and breast, to remind us that Christ should be in our thinking, in our speaking, and in our loving. Carry that mindset around with you. Choose a text to remind you of the passage you have been praying about: e.g., 'The Son of Man has nowhere to lay his head'; 'No one who puts has hand to the plough and looks back is fit for the kingdom of God.'

Prayer:

> Be gracious, Lord, to us whom you have called
> to follow your Beloved Son,
> and in your kindness increase your grace within us,
> so that strong in faith, hope and love,
> we may ever follow him faithfully,
> and accept his way of peace and love.
> We ask this through the same Christ our Lord. Amen.

Session 11: The Good Samaritan (Luke 10:25-37)

1. FOCUS
Focus the mind and heart on the presence of the Lord. For suggestions see Introduction p 18, or Session 1 p 26.

Prayer:

> Lord God, you are compassion and love. You have called us to love you, to love ourselves, and to love our neighbour, and to do so with all our heart and strength. Lord, you know how often we fail in love, and you know we can never make it on our own. So we ask you to pour the gifts of the Holy Spirit into our hearts, that the Spirit may help us to hear the word of Jesus, and to put it into practice, with head, and heart, and hands. We ask this through Christ our Lord. Amen.

2. FAMILIARISATION
This is a familiar story, so try to read it with fresh eyes. Take care to observe the setting for the parable, the question addressed to Jesus, and how he deals with it by getting the questioner to answer his own question. This provokes a further question, which Jesus answers by telling a story. Then Jesus asks a question, and when it is answered correctly, he says: Right, do that! Close your eyes and go over the sequence in your mind.

The setting: finding life.

> 10:25 Just then a lawyer stood up to test Jesus.
> 'Teacher,' he said, 'What must I do to inherit eternal life?'
> 26 He said to him, 'What is written in the law?
> What do you read there?'
> 27 He answered,
> 'You shall love the Lord your God with all your heart,
> and with all your soul, and with all your strength,
> and with all your mind (Deut 6:5);
> and your neighbour as yourself.' (Lev 19:18).
> 28 And he said to him,
> 'You have given the right answer; do this, and you will live.'

The parable: showing compassion

> 29 But wanting to justify himself, he asked Jesus,

'And who is my neighbour?'
30 Jesus replied,
'A man was going down from Jerusalem to Jericho,
and fell into the hands of robbers, who stripped him,
beat him, and went away, leaving him half dead.
31 Now by chance a priest was going down that road;
and when he saw him, he passed by on the other side.
32 So likewise a Levite, when he came to the place
and saw him, passed by on the other side.
33 But a Samaritan while travelling came near him,
and when he saw him, he was moved with pity.
34 He went to him and bandaged his wounds,
having poured oil and wine on them.
Then he put him on his own animal, brought him to an inn,
and took care of him.
35 The next day he took out two denarii,
gave them to the innkeeper, and said,
'Take care of him; and when I come back,
I will repay you whatever more you spend.'

How to be a neighbour
36 'Which of these three, do you think, was a neighbour
to the man who fell into the hands of robbers?'
37 He said, 'The one who showed him mercy.'
Jesus said to him, 'Go and do likewise.'

2.1 Background
The background is offered as a help to familiarisation, which in turn will aid our reflection on the text. Group leaders should become familiar with it before taking a group session. All participants in a group session are encouraged to read the text and the background notes before coming to the session.

2.1.1 The setting. The parable is part of the instruction to disciples as they accompany Jesus to Jerusalem. The immediate context is the question put to Jesus by an expert on the Law, asking what he must do to inherit eternal life. Jesus turns the question back to him, and he responds with the two fold commandment to love (really three-fold) from Deuteronomy 6:5 (love of God) and Leviticus 19:18 (love of neighbour as oneself). Jesus agrees with his answer: 'Do this, and you will live.' The lawyer's second question: 'Who is my neighbour?' becomes the occasion of the parable.

2.1.2 The command to love: In Mark and Matthew it is Jesus who first puts the command to love God together with the command to love neighbour as oneself. It is not clear whether the Jewish Rabbis had already done this. The quotation from Deut 6:5 is not exact, adding to with all your heart, soul, strength, the extra phrase 'with all your mind'. Thomas Groome (*What makes us Catholic?* Harper 2002) says the love of God has to engage our heads (all your mind), our hearts (heart and soul), and our hands (strength). The old Catechism question, 'Why did God make us?' was answered: 'To know, love and serve God in this life …'

2.1.3 The Parable: Note that Jesus does not give the lawyer the definition he wants. The question put to Jesus is, 'Who is my neighbour?' ('Who am I expected to love?' The context in Leviticus refers to the people of Israel only.) Jesus tells a story and asks, 'Who was a neighbour to the man who was robbed?' The question is now, 'How can I be a neighbour?' rather than finding a definition of 'neighbour'. 'Love does not begin by defining its objects: it discovers them … The point of the parable is that if a man has love in his heart, it will tell him who his neighbour is.' (T. W. Manson)

2.1.4 Samaritans: Luke in Acts records the conversion of many Samaritans to Christianity. Samaritans figure regularly in Luke (e.g. the Samaritan village, 9:52-56; the ten lepers, 17:11-19). The Samaritans were people of the Northern Kingdom intermarried with Gentile settlers, and not accepted by the Jews as part of the People of God. It makes the parable all the more striking that the one who acts as neighbour, presumably to a Jew, is a Samaritan.

2.1.5 Priest and Levite pass by the 'half-dead' victim of violence. The reason may have been their rules about uncleanness coming from touching a dead body, which would debar them from worship (Numbers 19:11-16). Jesus is implicitly calling into question the putting of ritual laws before humanity to those in need.

2.1.6 Symbolism? It has been suggested that certain words in the parable are capable of a symbolic interpretation. So in v 27 the work 'mercy' (Greek *eleos* representing Hebrew *hesed*) may be the great quality of God, made visible in Jesus, so that some say Jesus is the real 'Good Samaritan'. Going further, the inn has been interpreted as the church, to which the Good Samaritan brings us for healing, and the wine and oil represent the sacraments. But most modern commentators do not recommend this 'allegorising' of the parable (trying to make multiple points of comparison rather than looking at the main point the story is trying to make).

2.1.7 Martha and Mary (10:38-42): I do not think it is coincidence that Luke places Jesus' visit to Martha and Mary immediately after the Good Samaritan story. Jesus on his way to Jerusalem on his exodus journey receives hospitality from Martha and Mary. Martha prepares a meal, like a good hostess – surely an example of the practical love that Jesus calls for in the Good Samaritan episode. Yet we know that helping others can require sensitivity to the real needs of the person, love with the head as well as the heart and hands. Mary sits at the feet of Jesus and listens to his word. Martha would like to listen to Jesus also, but 'is distracted about much serving' (*diakonia*, which later becomes a theological word for serving the Lord and his people). Jesus gently tells her that 'only one thing – one course? – is necessary', and that Mary is doing the better thing at this time. What does Jesus really need at this point of his journey to Jerusalem? An elaborate meal, or a listening ear? Mary sees his need for more than bread. So practical love, love in action, has at times to give way to prayerful listening to the word. Prayer and action support and nourish each other, and there is a time for both. Martha and Mary are capable of both, just as we all are. But we do not always get the balance right.

3. REFLECTION

Take a period of silence to reflect on the text. We are going to use our Key Words to aid reflection, but for the moment just let the whole story make its impact on you. Group leaders might like to ask volunteers to share their initial impressions with the group.

3.1 Journey: We tend to think of neighbours as those who live close to us, the rest are strangers. If we follow Jesus on the road, he teaches us to show practical love to those we meet who may be in need. To pass by on the other side is a temptation of the modern world: do not get involved, keep out of it! Involvement means risk. It is a risky business following Jesus on his exodus journey. Only love will keep us going. But it can be a lonely journey if we remain aloof from all the people we meet.

3.2 Joy: Jesus knows it will nourish and mature us as persons to show practical love and come out of our isolation. Those who have suffered greatly have found that it helps to get involved in other people's suffering; it becomes healing for ourselves. We find hope in Jesus' teaching about the love of God for us, allowing us to respond. Hope also comes from the caring we have received from others (think of examples). Jesus assures us, 'What you do for one of my brothers/sisters, you do for me.' (Mt 25:40).

3.3 Personal: The theoretical question about love of neighbour is made personal and practical in the parable. We can identify with both the victim and the rescuer in the parable – sometimes also with those who pass by. Note how Jesus gets the lawyer to answer his own questions, even getting him to say the Samaritan was a good neighbour, though he can't get himself to use the name 'Samaritan'. Jesus tries to get us to answer our own questions also – love is also of the head, as well as heart and hands.

3.4 Challenge: Well, yes! We are challenged to the three loves, of God, self and neighbour, and to love with head, heart and hands. Challenged to practical love of those whom we meet who are in need, to show mercy, compassion, though it may cost us emotional involvement, time or money. 'What you do to one of these … you do to me.' It does not just apply to strangers. Some are more courteous and charming to strangers than to their own families. We are not to ignore the emotional, spiritual and physical needs of our own families.

4. RESPONSE
Avoid the temptation to go straight to feeling guilty about all the chances we missed to play the Good Samaritan. With yourself and others, begin with affirmation of the times you did well:

Jesus sees as done for himself anything we do for others. So, parents, think of all you have done for your families; husbands and wives, for each other, uncles and aunts, brothers and sisters, for others. Thank God for what he has allowed you to do, and for the 'growing up' that it brought you. Then examine the conscience about how we get involved with, or stay aloof from, others who are in trouble. Is it any different from getting involved with Jesus, or staying aloof from him? Now only very great people, like St Paul, can be all things to everyone, but pray for the grace to do things for some of those we meet, whose need we can see. Pray for a listening ear, for a ready smile to reassure the timid, for wisdom to know where we can help, and where we had better look for professional advice. We may become overwhelmed with the myriad needs of the world, but we will find that it is with the people in our lives already, or the ones we meet daily, that most opportunities to show practical love occur. Pray for the grace to see where we can help. Pray for the skill to do it. Pray for all who have given us practical, loving help in our lives. Above all, pray for love, for the love of God in our hearts, because love must be the motive, if we are to follow Jesus.

5. CONTEMPLATION

In spite of the danger of turning a parable into an allegory, mentioned above, I suggest it is a good thing to keep in our minds that Jesus himself is the great 'Good Samaritan', the one who has taken upon himself the fallen and wounded human race, and taken good care of us at great expense to himself. He has cared for us in the past, he cares for us now through his sacramental healing and nourishment of us, and he will always be with us. So walk in his presence, knowing you are loved and cared for. Choose a text to live with, and let it simmer in your consciousness; e.g. 'This do and you shall live'.

Prayer:

> Lord, help us to pray, but let our prayer give us the will and the strength to show love in action. And please, Lord, help us to guide and nourish our acts of love done in your name by real listening to your word, that we may try to build your kingdom and not our own. Amen.

Session 12: Sharing Your Blessings (Luke 12:13-34)

1. FOCUS
Focus the mind and heart on the presence of God. For suggestions see Introduction p 18, or Session 1 p 26.

Prayer:

> Lord God our Father, we have learned from St Luke to praise you for the blessings we have received. You have blessed us with gifts of the Spirit, and with material gifts. Help us to use our material gifts with joy, but with generosity. Teach us not to seek for more than we can reasonably use, and teach us to share with others what we have over. In a world of greed and consumption, where it is seen as good business to corner the market to keep prices high, where food is dumped while half the world starves, help us to remember the option for the poor, and to try to be a sign in our world of Jesus' call to share with the poor. Amen.

2. FAMILIARISATION
This is a long text, so it may take some time to become familiar with it. The sequence is: Jesus finds occasion to warn against the desire to have many possessions; then he tells a parable as illustration, the foolish rich man who is not going to live to enjoy his possessions; this is followed by the lovely passage about trust in God and giving alms.

The setting
> 13 Someone in the crowd said to him,
> 'Teacher, tell my brother
> to divide the family inheritance with me.'
> 14 But he said to him,
> 'Friend, who set me to be a judge or arbitrator over you?'
> 15 And he said to them,
> 'Take care! Be on your guard against all kinds of greed:
> for one's life does not consist in the abundance of possessions.'

The parable
> 16 Then he told them a parable:
> 'The land of a rich man produced abundantly.

17 And he thought to himself,
'What should I do, for I have no place to store my crops.'
18 Then he said, 'I will do this:
I will pull down my barns and build larger ones,
and there I will store all my grain and my goods.
19 And I will say to my soul,
'Soul, you have ample goods laid up for many years;
relax, eat, drink and be merry.'
20 But God said to him, 'You fool!
This very night your life will be demanded of you.
And the things you have prepared, whose will they be?'
21 So it is with those who store up treasures for themselves
and are not rich towards God.'

Trust in God the Father, who knows our needs.
22 He said to his disciples,
'Therefore I tell you, do not worry about your life,
what you will eat, or about your body, what you will wear.
23 For life is more than food, and the body more than clothing.
24 Consider the ravens: they neither sow nor reap,
they have neither storehouse nor barn,
and yet God feeds them.
Of how much more value are you than the birds!
25 And can any of you by worrying
add a single hour to your span of life?
26 If then you are not able to do so small a thing as that,
why do you worry about the rest?
27 Consider the lilies, how they grow:
they neither toil nor spin;
yet I tell you, even Solomon in all his glory
was not clothed like one of these.
28 But if God so clothes the grass of the field,
which is alive today and tomorrow is thrown into the oven,
how much more will he clothe you – you of little faith!
29 And do not keep striving for what you are to eat
and what you are to drink, and do not keep worrying.
30 For it is the nations of the world
that strive after all these things,
and your Father knows that you need them.

31 Instead, strive for his kingdom,
and these things will be given to you as well.
32 Do not be afraid, little flock,
for it is your Father's good pleasure to give you the kingdom.
33 Sell your possessions and give alms.
Make purses for yourselves that do not wear out,
an unfailing treasure in heaven,
where no thief comes near and no moth destroys.
34 For where your treasure is, there your heart will be also.

2.1 Background

This background is offered to help with understanding the text, and so to make reflection easier. Group leaders should familiarise themselves with it before group sessions. All participants in a group session are encouraged to read the text and the background notes before coming to the meeting.

2.1.1 *Luke's social teaching:* Luke's beatitudes are more direct and particular than those in Matthew. 'Blessed are you who are poor, for yours is the kingdom of God … Woe to you who are rich, for you have received your consolation' (6:20, 24). Jesus does not advocate poverty for itself – we are to help the poor to overcome it. Neither are riches evil in themselves: it's the attitudes they bring that matter. Preoccupation with money leads to selfishness, makes one deaf to God's word, over-concerned with pleasure and outward appearance, indifferent to others and to eternity. Jesus calls for sharing what one does not need, giving up what stifles the spirit, finding security not in money or status, but in God.

2.1.2 *Jesus' teaching* on this occasion begins from a personal encounter (though he refuses to get involved in a family dispute). There follows a general warning against greed (*pleonexia*, desire for more than one needs), which is then illustrated by a parable (12:16-21) about a farmer who hoards everything for himself. It is all positively developed in the great passage about trust in God's goodness (12:22-34), which Luke shares with Matthew (6:25-33), while giving it his own particular colouring. This he does by v 33: 'Sell your possessions and give alms', and above all by setting it in the journey to Jerusalem (in Matthew it is part of the Sermon on the Mount).

2.1.3 The parable is addressed to the crowd, which in Luke is usually positive towards Jesus, warning his hearers against keeping everything for oneself. The section on 'Trust in God' is addressed to the disciples, therefore part of their instruction as they follow Jesus on the road to Jerusalem. The advice to let go and trust in God is particularly relevant to disciples following Jesus, who will lovingly surrender himself to the Father's will on Calvary: 'Father, into your hands I give myself' (23:46). There are two kinds of call to disciples in St Luke. Some are called to give up everything, 'Sell all you own and distribute the money to the poor', (the rich young man, 18:22), and become 'full-time' followers of Jesus. Others are to stay at home with their families, become witnesses where they live and work (like Zacchaeus, 19:1-10). But every disciple is called to develop attitudes of trust in God, sharing of one's surplus, concern for the destitute. The people addressed originally in the section on trust in God were not the very poor, but those who have something to give up, and Luke makes the call more urgent because Jesus on the road to Jerusalem is seeking more people to commit themselves to full-time discipleship.

2.1.4 'Blessed are you who are poor' (6:20): 'Blessed' not just because of poverty, but because the poor know their need of God, and are therefore more open to the gifts of God, particularly the gifts of the Kingdom (6:20: 'for yours is the kingdom of God'). Jesus' greatest difficulty, then and now, is to get through to the self-sufficient, who do not know their poverty, and are indifferent to the call to open up to God.

3. REFLECTION
Take a few minutes to reflect quietly on the impact the text has made on you. Is it heartening, or scary, too demanding, refreshing, challenging? Group leaders may wish to invite participants to share briefly their initial impressions of the passage.

3.1 Journey: It was recommended of old that on the journey of life we should see things '*sub specie aeternitatis*' (from the prospect of eternity). Not just 'pie in the sky when you die', but learning here and now the virtues which are 'of heaven' – caring for each other, sharing our surplus, giving ourselves into the care of God.

110

So read the parable of the man who plans for the future with no thought for anyone else, or for God. Be 'rich towards God' for 'one's life does not consist in the abundance of possessions'. As we get older, we have to give up doing things that we can no longer do: is this life's training ground for the time when we have to say with Jesus, 'Father, into your hands I give myself'? To receive ourselves back enriched by new life?

3.2 *Joy:* What makes us bless the Lord in this passage? What do we find life-giving? In truth some of it is disturbing, making strong calls on our generosity. Yet as we reflect on his words, we see the great care of Jesus for us, like a parent's care that a child may not grow up grasping and selfish. Jesus knows that generous giving is not just insurance with God for the future, but freedom now: the simple life frees us from anxiety and care, opens us up to each other. Jesus says: 'Be on your guard', 'Do not worry about your life'; 'Of how much more value are you than the birds', 'Do not keep worrying', 'Do not be afraid'. And the most consoling phrase of all: 'Your Father knows!' *Lord, we rejoice in your care for us; help our faltering trust.*

3.3 *Personal:* This teaching arises out of a personal encounter with a man who brings a problem to Jesus. He does not get the answer he wants, of course. Lord, teach us to know our true needs. Take the section on 'Trust in God' (22-34), and see it as addressed to you, Theophilus/a, and ask what Jesus is trying to say to you personally. Perhaps we have a problem of finance dominating our waking hours, or it may be health, fear of death, a flawed image of a God who is more demanding than loving, or some other piece of baggage from the past. Take the problem to Jesus and try to hear what he is saying. Do you feel his concern for you? 'Of how much more value are you than the birds' (v 24).

3.4 *Challenge:* There is no doubting the challenge in these verses. If I choose to be a follower of Jesus on the road to Jerusalem and to the Father, then I positively cannot live a lifestyle which is a betrayal of that calling. So I must guard against greed, share my resources, strive for his kingdom, give alms, trust in the Father's goodness and love for me. We know how anxious we can get, how often we are tempted to put our security in money or possessions. The lure of the advertiser is hard to evade: the things that are going to make us happier, more beautiful, healthier, more popular, better entertained, all so attractively presented. We are challenged to look inside to find our true worth, not based on which car we drive, designer clothes, the latest in gadgets, but in being sons/daughters of God and brothers/sisters to all God's people.

4. RESPONSE

Where my treasure is, there will my heart be also. Where is my treasure? Are you my hope and riches, Lord, or am I hopelessly entangled in too many material possessions? Lord, I give thanks for the gift of life, health, peace of mind, for your love and the blessings I have received from you. Teach me gratitude, keep me from being grasping and possessive. Give me joy in sharing with others. Help me to see the needs of others. Keep me from trying to be my own security against all dangers: you are my security! I am in your care, come what may! Increase my faith in you. I am rich with your blessings. Help me to simplify my life. Help me to make space for you, and for prayer. Help me to make time for others who may need me. Help me to rejoice that my heavenly Father knows my real needs better that I do. Help me to resist the magpie impulse to acquire the latest fashionable possession. Give me joy in the beauty of your world. Help me to be conscious of my obligation to take care of that beauty, to be 'greener' in my thinking and in my use of the world's resources.

5. CONTEMPLATION

Look at the lilies of the field, the ravens – or as close as you can get to them. Appreciate the things around you, and the people. Be aware of the simple things we take for granted, and enjoy them. They are signs of the Father's love. St Francis saw everything around him tinged with the divine, because Jesus took our flesh and lived among us. Pick a phrase to live in your consciousness till it becomes a part of you: e.g. 'Life is more than food, and the body more than clothing'; 'It is your Father's good pleasure to give you the kingdom'.

Prayer:

Lord, I need peace within, I need to count my real blessings, I need to see the concerns of my brothers and sisters, I need to believe that the will of God for me is always for my good. Help me to learn trust, contentment, hope in your goodness. Free me from useless yearnings, from anxiety, help me to feel your presence deep within me. Give me strength to reach out to others and to share my gifts with them. Amen.

Session 13: Lost and Found: The Prodigal Son
(Luke 15:1-3, 11-32)

1. FOCUS
Focus the mind and heart in the presence of the Lord. For suggestions see Introduction p 18, or Session 1 p 26.

Prayer:
> Lord Jesus, in spite of the gifts you have given us, and in spite of our good intentions, we often lose our way, and squander your gifts. Give us the grace always to seek forgiveness, to return to our Father's house. You spoke about the joy in heaven when a sinner repents, and so we ask for a strong faith in our Father's welcoming love. Help us to open our minds and hearts to your great story of a father's love and forgiveness, of a son's homecoming, that we may always know the welcome that awaits us when we return to God our Father. Amen.

2. FAMILIARISATION
Sometimes our difficulty is that a story is too familiar. This is one of the great stories if you read it with fresh eyes. Note the introduction, vv 1-3, which helps you to know why Jesus told stories of loss and finding. A loving father loses two sons, and at the end has got one wanderer back and lost the one who never left. Read it a few times and then close your eyes and retell it to yourself.

Introduction: welcoming sinners
> 15:1 Now all the tax collectors and sinners
> were coming near to listen to him.
> 2 And the Pharisees and the scribes were grumbling and saying,
> 'This fellow welcomes sinners and eats with them.'
> 3 So he told them this parable:
> [*here follow the lost sheep, vv 3-7, and the lost coin, vv 8-10.*]

The Prodigal Son
> 11 Then Jesus said, There was a man who had two sons.
> 12 The younger of them said to his father,
> 'Father, give me the share of the property

that will belong to me.'
So he divided his property between them.

Lost

13 A few days later the younger son gathered all he had
and travelled to a distant country,
and there he squandered his property on dissolute living.
14 When he had spent everything,
a severe famine took place throughout that country,
and he began to be in need.
15 So he went and hired himself out
to one of the citizens of that country,
who sent him into his fields to feed the pigs.
16 He would gladly have filled himself
with the pods that the pigs were eating,
but no one gave him anything.

Found

17 And when he came to himself, he said,
'How many of my father's hired hands
have bread enough and to spare,
and here I am dying of hunger!
18 I will get up and go to my father, and I will say to him
'Father, I have sinned against heaven and before you.
19 I am no longer worthy to be called your son;
treat me as one of your hired hands.'
20 So he set off and went to his father.
But while he was still far off,
his father saw him and was filled with compassion;
he ran and put his arms around him and kissed him.
21 Then the son said to him,
'Father, I have sinned against heaven and before you;
I am no longer worthy to be called your son.'
22 But the father said to his slaves, 'Quickly, bring out a robe
– the best one –and put it on him;
put a ring on his finger and sandals on his feet.
23 And get the fatted calf and kill it, and let us eat and celebrate;
24 for this son of mine was dead and is alive again,
he was lost and is found.'
And they began to celebrate.

Found and lost
    25 Now his elder son was in the field;
and when he came and approached the house,
he heard music and dancing.
26 He called one of the slaves
and asked him what was going on.
27 He replied, 'Your brother has come,
and your father has killed the fatted calf,
because he has got him back safe and sound.'
28 Then he became angry and refused to go in.
His father came out and began to plead with him.
29 But he answered his father, 'Listen!
For all these years I have been working like a slave for you
and I have never disobeyed your command;
yet you have never given me even a young goat
so that I might celebrate with my friends.
30 But when this son of yours came back,
who has devoured your property with prostitutes,
you killed the fatted calf for him!'
31 Then the father said to him,
'Son, you are always with me, and all that is mine is yours.
32 But we had to celebrate and rejoice,
because this brother of yours was dead and has come to life,
he was lost and has been found.'

2.1 Background
Leaders of groups should be familiar with the background before taking
a group. Others are strongly encouraged to read the text and the back-
ground notes before coming to a group session.

2.1.1 Luke Chapter 15 has a unity of theme, with an introduction
(15:1-3), which explains why Jesus addresses these three parables to the Pharisees and scribes, who are not hearing the message. They are of course addressed to all of us who fail to hear
the message about God's extravagant love for his children. We
have three parables of losing and the joy of finding, joy that
must be celebrated: the lost sheep (15:4-7), the lost coin (15:8-10),
and the lost ('prodigal' or wasteful) son, or perhaps better, the
lost sons (15:11-32). This chapter has been called 'the heart' of

Luke's gospel (Ramaroson, quoted by Fitzmeyer, vol 2, p 1071). It is really too long for our purposes, even the parable of the lost sons alone, yet it is so characteristic of Luke (only Luke has the lost coin and lost son stories), that we want to pray about it. We will look closely at the introduction, and at the major themes of the parable of the lost sons.

2.1.2 The Introduction (vv.1-3): Tax-collectors and sinners come 'to hear Jesus' (to take his message to heart). Pharisees and scribes hear, but grumble about the company he keeps (like the Israelites in the desert). They say, and they intend to dismiss Jesus' claims to speak for God, 'This fellow welcomes sinners and eats with them.' No prophet of God, in their thinking, would associate with sinners, who are, by definition, far from God. Yet in reality these 'sinners' are listening to Jesus and re-joicing in the message that gives them hope and joy, while the 'righteous' ones stay aloof. Jesus' parables illustrate that they do not really know God, if they think he is not interested in finding the lost. We have already seen this illustrated in the episode of Simon the Pharisee and the sinful woman (session 7, 7:36-50), and it has been highlighted in 14:16-24, the parable of the banquet, to which the invited guests would not come, so the banquet was opened to 'the poor, the crippled, the blind and the lame'.

2.1.3 The Loving Father: Some would prefer this title for the para-ble, even 'the prodigal father', for he is extravagantly generous, wasteful with his love, certainly in the eyes of his elder son. This teaches us the utter extravagance of God the Father's love for his lost children. The one who experiences the loss is in a sense the chief actor in each parable, with a focus on sadness at the loss, determination to find the lost, the joyful welcome when the lost is found, and the need to celebrate the joy of finding with others. This joyful welcome, says Jesus, is but a pale reflection of the joy in heaven, when a sinner returns to God. Others are invited to join the celebration. The elder son in the third parable refuses the invitation, representing the leaders of Israel, the favoured sons, who are unwilling to hear the message of Jesus, and to re-joice in the return of sinners to God. Readers of the third parable are meant to identify with the lost son, though surprisingly many identify with the elder son, without realising that he was lost as well. So it seems better to keep the traditional title which focuses on the son.

2.1.4 More than one way to be lost: There are two patterns of becoming lost in the parable. The more obvious pattern is represented by the younger son. He has a fine home, a loving father, but he wants to leave, be independent, find freedom. With a lack of feeling for his family, he goes to a far country, and squanders his inheritance, as many a son has done. He suffers humiliation and degradation, but 'comes to himself' (v 17) – that moment of graced insight, without which no repentance is possible. He returns home, chastened, ready to accept a lesser status, but is received with joy and feasting by his father, who speaks no word of blame.

The elder son demonstrates, not the dramatic departure for a distant land, but the gradual drift away without ever leaving home, dutiful observance concealing growing anger and bitterness of heart. When the younger brother returns, the anger erupts, and he is unable to accept him back as a brother, or his father's invitation to celebrate. He does not 'come to himself'. The parable ends with 'unfinished business', to give us food for thought. Will the elder son think better? Will the father's love be able to reach out to him? We need to reflect on our own lives, see whether one or other, or even both, of these patterns fits into our own life story.

2.1.5 Biblical pattern: There is a well-known biblical pattern, from as early as the Book of Judges (2:11-19), describing the relationship of the Israelites to God. The cycle begins with the people's fervour and their gratitude to God for his deliverance of them. But this fervour cools over time and becomes carelessness, indifference, even betrayal. Then comes a crisis; the people need deliverance again, and must turn to God in repentance and prayer, and he saves them, and they are grateful – and the cycle begins again! Can you identify this cycle in your own spiritual life? We constantly need the grace to 'come to ourselves'.

3. REFLECTION
Take a period of quiet reflection, identifying areas of the text which speak to you. Group leaders may wish to invite volunteers to share briefly their initial response to the text.

3.1 Journey: His physical journey to a distant land in a way symbolises the younger son's distancing of himself from family ties and affections. In his case exile and high living, then poverty and famine, finally his being reduced to taking the meanest job for a Jew, feeding pigs, represent the journey away from home. In the case of the elder son, drift and hardness of heart, probably an inability to communicate with his father ('You have never given me even a young goat, so that I might celebrate' – probably he could never ask for it), lead to his distancing of himself from the father, without leaving home. 'Coming to oneself' is needed for the journey home – sometimes, alas, hitting rock bottom, where there is nowhere to go but up. The elder son does not realise his need for repentance, to the younger son it is all too obvious. We all need to pray for the grace to realise our need, to 'come to ourselves', and to act on the realisation. Spend a little time reflecting on your own experience, how you felt when you were 'lost', how you came to your senses, how you felt when you were welcomed home.

3.2 Joy: Each of the three parables has the same theme of joy in heaven because a sinner was lost and is found. The father says, 'We had to celebrate and rejoice because this brother of yours was dead and has come to life; he was lost and has been found' (v 32). Do you remember the joy of forgiveness? Has it passed over into doubts about that forgiveness? Is it ever possible that we, the ones welcomed back, could ourselves refuse to join the celebration, because we are unable to forgive ourselves, or are not quite sure of being forgiven? The father says, 'We *had to* celebrate and rejoice.' So, especially if you owe yourself some joy that you refused to accept in the past, celebrate your forgiveness and enjoy being clothed in the splendour of the new life of the risen Christ, and nourished at the banquet of the Eucharist. Are we able to rejoice in other people returning to God and finding forgiveness? It is only if we remember our personal joy that we will be able to really rejoice in other people's forgiveness.

3.3 Personal: The story is one of family relationships, close, cool, indifferent, broken, restored. The younger son makes his inner journey from heedlessness, reckless selfishness, to finding his inner self, humility, confession of guilt, return to his father, finding joyful welcome. The elder son allows bitterness to build up inside him, blames his brother for leaving him extra work, is secretly angry with his father. The anger explodes when his young brother returns, but he cannot call him brother –'this son of yours'. Only the elder brother says the prodigal squandered his money on prostitutes. He is unable to share the joy of the celebration, has no welcome or openness.

The story is also about our personal relationship to God. Where are we on the scale? Do we really trust God our Father to be welcoming when we need to return and find forgiveness? Do we see the God we have experienced in this father who allows his son to go, gives him freedom, though he fears it will be misused, waits patiently for his return, never ceases to love him, welcomes him back without a word of reproach, clothes him in splendour and celebrates his coming back to life from the dead. Is this 'our God'? Or do we need to enlarge our picture of God's unceasing love and total forgiveness? Could we be guilty of not being able to talk to our Father, as was probably the case of the elder son with his father? Does your image of God need to be rethought? Is it distorted by poorly informed teaching in your past, or by bad experiences of authority figures? We need to forgive those people, let it go, refuse to allow past hurts to make us bitter. We do not have to be perfect to be loved. Allow the Father's love to heal and renew you. To nourish a more trustful relationship with God we need to keep on praying. We need to remember that cycle (see 2.1.5 above), where fervour and gratitude become coolness and indifference, and we need to be rekindled in personal prayer from the heart.

3.4 *Challenge:* Our challenge is to return to God each time we drift/run away from him, and to trust that we will receive generous forgiveness. If we have worries about the past, we need to face up to them honestly, and be rid of our burden of guilt once for all. Some of us drag burdens of guilt behind us for years and years, often because of misinformation, upbringing, a poor self image because of how we were treated by others, knowingly or unknowingly. This generous God does not wish us to be so burdened. His forgiveness is total. Our challenge is to have trust in God's unconditional love, and then to be forgiving towards others.

We need to forgive ourselves, and others. Harbouring grudges, even if there has been good cause, is the surest way to destroy our inner joy, bringing only bitterness that corrodes our hearts. Jesus said we must forgive and pray for those who have hurt us; there is no other medicine for hurts. We must hold doors open to reconciliation and not remain aloof. This will allow us to share in the joy of the Lord. Many parents have had to live the experience of the father in the story, seeing their children go away, lose their faith, fail in their relationships. Like the father, keep doors open, pray for them, do not give up hope. Invite them home when that is possible. Be sure that they see that you are alive, filled with God's life, and be a living invitation to them to rejoin the family of God.

4. RESPONSE

This must be very personal to each of us, and so I will be brief. We have all been there – felt lost, estranged, helpless, reckless, guilty, wasteful ('The love that we have wasted, O God of love, renew'). We can spend time fruitfully going over our personal histories of forgiveness and resentments, and how we dealt with them, or still have to deal with them. But this story points us in one main direction: to rejoice in the prodigal love of God our Father, to celebrate the wonder of the Father's generous love. Pray for an enriched image of God. Our feelings may have been badly hurt by authority figures in the past, people who mistook sternness for love, people who could never quite be pleased with us, who gave us scant praise and damaged the image of the Father God in us. Forgive those people, and refuse to be tied down by the image of God they gave you. Thank Jesus for his gift of re-imaging God our Father for us, thank him for 'the love of God made visible in Jesus Christ our Lord' (Romans 8:39, JB translation). Give thanks to God our Father for his love and forgiveness, for being always the God of new chances, for sending his beloved Son to call us back to himself in love. Give thanks for the availability of the Sacrament of Reconciliation, and resolve to use it well, concentrating more on the grace of forgiveness than on fear of admitting your need for healing. Then you can pray about the forgiveness you need now, about the times you have already experienced it. Pray about the people you need to forgive, about those you have forgiven and who have forgiven you. Pray for trust. Above all, pray for readiness to accept the Father's invitation to the banquet. What if we, like the elder son, were not able to accept, not able to go in to the celebration?

5. CONTEMPLATION

Keep the Father's joy and welcome alive in your mind and heart. Intend and expect to find joy in God's love and forgiveness. Cultivate a forgiving heart. Pray for the wanderers. Feed your children's faith lovingly. Choose a text to live with and to remind you of the joy and celebration of the lost being found. 'This man welcomes sinners and eats with them.' 'He came to himself and said … I will get up and go to my father.' 'There is joy in the presence of the angels of God over one sinner who repents' (15:10).

Prayer:

Lord God our Father, we are lost until found by you, dead until you give us your life. We rejoice in your welcoming love, which receives us back whenever we stray. We pray for all who wander from you in error, ignorance or malice, and we rejoice in the return of the wanderers, with all the angels in heaven. Help us always to trust your goodness and love, made visible to us in Jesus Christ our Lord. Amen.

Session 14: Entering Jerusalem (Luke 19:28-48)

1. FOCUS

Focus the mind and heart on the presence of God. For suggestions see Introduction p 18, or Session 1 p 26.

Prayer:

> Lord, your holy city, Jerusalem, is a place of glory and sadness, 'the place where you gave your name a home', where your plans for your people have often been hindered and delayed by the blindness and hardness of heart of your people. We have followed your Son in his courageous journey to the Holy City to meet his destiny, which will bring him through suffering to your presence in glory. Help us to learn from his joy in doing your will, from his courage in facing sorrow and death, and grace us with the same joy and courage when we one day face the journey to the heavenly Jerusalem, to live in your presence. We ask this through Christ our Lord. Amen.

2. FAMILIARISATION

Read the text a few times until you become familiar with it. With a long text like this, let the sequence of events become clear, but it is not necessary to try to pray about it all at once; focus your prayer on the first section for now, and gradually expand your attention to the other parts.

Jesus reaches the city of his destiny
19:28 After he had said this, he went on ahead,
going up to Jerusalem.
29 And when he had come near Bethphage and Bethany,
at a place called the Mount of Olives,
he sent two of his disciples,
30 saying, 'Go into the village ahead of you,
and as you enter it you will find tied there
a colt that has never been ridden. Untie it and bring it here.
31 If anyone asks you, "Why are you untying it?'
just say this, "The Lord needs it".'
32   So those who were sent departed
and found it as he had told them.

33 As they were untying the colt, its owners asked them,
'Why are you untying the colt?'
34 They said, 'The Lord needs it.'
35 Then they brought it to Jesus;
and after throwing their cloaks on the colt,
they set Jesus on it.
36 As he rode along,
people kept spreading their cloaks on the road.
37 As he was now approaching
the path down from the Mount of Olives,
the whole multitude of the disciples
began to praise God joyfully, with a loud voice,
for all the deeds of power that they had seen, saying,
38 'Blessed is the king who comes in the name of the Lord!
Peace in heaven, and glory in the highest heaven!'
39 Some of the Pharisees in the crowd said to him,
'Teacher, order your disciples to stop.'
40 He answered,
'I tell you, if these were silent, the stones would shout out.'

Jesus weeps over the city
41 As he came near and saw the city, he wept over it,
42 saying, 'If you, even you, had only recognised on this day
the things that make for peace!
But now they are hidden from your eyes.
43 Indeed, the days will come upon you,
when your enemies will set up ramparts round you
and surround you, and hem you in on every side.
44 They will crush you to the ground,
you and your children within you,
and they will not leave within you one stone upon another;
because you did not recognise
the time of your visitation from God.'

Jesus cleanses the temple
45 Then he entered the temple,
and began to drive out those who were selling things there;
46 and he said, 'It is written,
"My house shall be a house of prayer,
but you have made it a den of robbers".'

Jesus' ministry of teaching in the temple.

47 Every day he was teaching in the temple.

The chief priests, the scribes, and the leaders of the people kept looking for a way to kill him;

48 but they did not find anything they could do,

for all the people were spellbound by what they heard.

2.1 Background

Group leaders should become familiar with the background before beginning a group session. All others who take part in group meetings are strongly encouraged to read the text and the background notes before coming to the meeting.

2.1.1 Geography: Jesus travels from Jericho, which is near the Jordan and well below sea-level, up to Jerusalem, which is on the central mountain range. When travellers emerge over the summit of the Mount of Olives, the city is spread out before them, with the valley of the brook Kedron in between, with the Golden Gate of the temple facing the Mount of Olives. Today it is still an impressive sight, with the Muslim Shrine, the Dome of the Rock marking with its golden dome the site of the Jewish temple, destroyed by the Romans in 70 AD. In between you are led to think of death and resurrection, since the eye can see a vast array of Jewish tombstones over bodies buried there to be close to the place where they believe the general resurrection will take place.

2.1.2 Jerusalem is the city of God, the place of destiny. Jesus is coming, a faithful Jew, to worship the Lord in Jerusalem at the Passover, a pilgrim feast, which all adult Jewish males were expected to attend. He had been brought here as a child by his parents and presented to the Lord in the temple (2:22-38). Simeon had welcomed the child with joy, and had prophesied, 'This child is destined for the falling and the rising of many in Israel, and to be a sign that will be opposed' (2:34), adding that a sword would pierce his mother's soul. He went again for the feast of the Passover (2:41-51) when he was 12 years old, the time when a Jewish boy celebrates his bar mitzvah, becoming a child of the Law. At that time he became engrossed in listening to the teaching of the Rabbis on the Law, and forgot to go home with the pilgrims from Galilee. To Mary and Joseph he said, 'Did you not know that I must be in my Father's house (*or about my Father's business*)' (2:49)

Luke has deliberately expanded the narrative of Jesus' journey to Jerusalem, begun at 9:51, and has repeated at regular intervals, like a background drumbeat, that Jesus was heading for Jerusalem. When warned about danger from Herod (Antipas), Jesus said, '... it is impossible for a prophet to be killed outside of Jerusalem. Jerusalem, Jerusalem, the city that kills the prophets and stones those who are sent to it! How often have I desired to gather your children together as a hen gathers her brood under her wings, and you were not willing! ... you will not see me until the time comes when you say, Blessed is the one who comes in the name of the Lord.' (13:33-35). Jesus comes to the end of the journey to Jerusalem with a mixture of joy and that sadness already noted in the above quotation, because Jerusalem does not realise the importance of the moment, nor its own coming tribulation.

2.1.3 Entry into Jerusalem: Jesus' intentions, upon his entry to Jerusalem, present a difficult and much discussed question. Later the Christian community saw it as his solemn Messianic statement, the Messiah being hailed and acclaimed as king as he entered his city. The riding on the donkey was interpreted as a deliberate fulfilment of Zechariah 9: 9. 'Rejoice greatly, O daughter Zion! Shout aloud, O daughter Jerusalem! O, your king comes to you, triumphant and victorious he is, humble and riding on a donkey, on a colt, the foal of a donkey.' Matthew (21:5) explicitly refers to this text, but Luke has only some possible verbal links with the Septuagint Greek translation. There was a Messianic interpretation of this text by Jewish Rabbis, though scholars differ about whether it was known in the time of Jesus – and therefore available to Jesus – or only later. Pilgrims arriving in Jerusalem were greeted with the salutation of Ps 118:26, 'Blessed is the one who comes in the name of the Lord. We bless you from the house of the Lord.' This salutation was undoubtedly addressed to Jesus, and the accompanying pilgrims from Galilee would have taken it up. Luke adds to the salutation the words 'the king', which might be seen as coming from Zechariah 9:9.

All things considered, I believe that it is safe to hold that Jesus was making a conscious statement that he was the Messiah, at least to his close disciples, a Messiah without pomp, who comes in peace, 'humble and riding on a donkey'. After all, he could have walked into Jerusalem, and the decision to ride on the donkey is very deliberate. Note that it was largely the Galilee pilgrims, including his own disciples ('the whole multitude of the disciples' v 37), who saluted him as 'the one [the king] who comes in the name of the Lord.' We have here Luke's answer to the question of John the Baptist, 'Are you the one who is to come?' (7:20), and to the question of Herod Antipas, 'Who is this about whom I hear such things?' (9:9)

2.1.4 Weeping over Jerusalem: Three times Jesus laments the fate of Jerusalem, here and two other times. Following the warning referred to in the paragraph above (2.1.2), Jesus adds, 'Jerusalem, Jerusalem ... how often have I desired to gather your children together as a hen gathers her brood under her wings, and you were not willing!'(13:34). And on the Way of the Cross, Jesus tells the weeping women not to weep for him, but for themselves: 'Daughters of Jerusalem, do not weep for me, but weep for yourselves and for your children' (23:28). A little church on the side of the Mount of Olives overlooking Jerusalem, with a roof shaped like a teardrop, is called *'Dominus flevit'*, 'The Lord wept', and commemorates the weeping over Jerusalem in our present passage. Jesus' compassion for Jerusalem and for its people is a regular theme in Luke.

2.1.5 Comparison with Mark: Luke follows Mark's narrative of these events, with his own changes, omissions and additions. These help us to see what Luke was trying to emphasise. They both have the cure of the blind man at Jericho (Mark 10:46-52, Luke 18:35-43) [those who allow Jesus to heal their blindness become his followers]; Luke adds the story of Zacchaeus (19:1-10), giving the purpose of his mission – 'to seek and save the lost'. Mark has Jesus entering Jerusalem, then going to the temple, looking around briefly, and retiring to Bethany (Mark 11:1-11). But in Luke, Jesus goes straight to the temple, after he has wept over the city (19:41-44, Luke's addition). Mark has the cursing of the fig tree, then the cleansing of the temple, then the finding of

the fig tree withered (Mark 10:12-24). Luke has Jesus immediately cleansing the temple (Luke 19:45-46, shorter than Mark), then
taking up his teaching ministry in the temple (19:47-48, continued through chapters 20-21). Luke therefore omits the fig tree al-
together and the return to Bethany. The focus of Luke's narrative therefore is Jesus coming to purify the temple (my Father's
house, 2:49), and carrying on his teaching ministry there – seen
as the fulfilment of the prophecy of Malachi 3:1-3: 'The Lord
whom you seek will suddenly come to his temple ... who can
endure the day of his coming, and who can stand when he appears? For he is like a refiner's fire ... and he will purify the descendants of Levi, until they present offerings to the Lord in
righteousness.' This was already hinted at in the Presentation
story (2:22-38). Luke tells about the cleansing of the temple very
briefly, and perhaps what Luke wants to emphasise is the mis-
use of the temple, which God intended to be a house of prayer.
Jesus comes to teach there, and restore it to its proper use. Note
that as elsewhere in Luke's narrative, 'the crowds' are not hostile, but 'spellbound by what they heard' (19:48), and this places
an obstacle to the plotting of 'the chief priests, the scribes, and
the leaders of the people', who were trying to find a way to kill
him.

3. REFLECTION
*Take a period of quiet reflection to digest the text. Group leaders may
wish to invite those who feel comfortable to share briefly what strikes
them initially about the passage.*

3.1 *Journey:* Jesus at last reaches Jerusalem, the city of his destiny,
along with his disciples. Jesus loves this city, and its temple, the
holy place of God's presence with his people. His arrival is only
a stage of the journey: Luke has already referred to his 'exodus'
(9:31), and his 'taking up' (9:51), so Jerusalem is the theatre
where the dramatic events of his death, resurrection and going
to the Father will take place. For the disciples who accompany
him, the arrival must have been a mixture of trepidation and excitement, as they saw the reception he received coming into the
city. The drama to come will severely test what they have
learned on the journey, and their loyalty to Jesus. We often think

we know what is coming and believe that we can deal with it. The reality is often much different, and we need to rely on prayer and the power of God, rather than our own powers.

3.2 *Joy:* There is a mixture of joy and sorrow in the passage. Pick out the joy and sorrow: e.g. v 37 is only in Luke: 'The whole multitude of the disciples began to praise God joyfully, with a loud voice.' In the following verses (38-40) Luke highlights the tremendous occasion, the Messiah reaching the city of his destiny. By contrast, vv 41-44 highlight Jesus' personal sadness that the people of Jerusalem fail to understand the meaning of what is happening and are unaware of the fate of the city. We share the emotions of Palm Sunday / Passion Sunday in our church celebrations, joy and acclamation that the Saviour arrives in Jerusalem to accomplish the work of our salvation, sadness that the way to accomplish it will cause Jesus such pain. Over all, however, we celebrate the wonder of our salvation, the cause of our deepest joy. Luke seems to be giving us the key to his editing of the whole passage in that v 37 (unique to himself): 'The whole multitude of the disciples began to praise God joyfully, with a loud voice, for all the deeds of power that they had seen.' Jesus approves of this joyful praise, for when some Pharisees told him to quieten his disciples, he said (v 40): 'I tell you, if these were silent, the stones would shout out.' There is something in the very nature of what is happening that demands joyful praise of God and acclamation of Jesus as the one who comes in God's name. That is consistent with the whole theme of joyful praise for the blessings of salvation, which runs through the gospel of Luke. No palm branches are mentioned in Luke, but we may stop for a moment and reflect on our feelings as Jesus is acclaimed 'the king who comes in the name of the Lord'.

3.3 *Personal:* Think about how this section is personal (a) for Jesus, (b) for us readers. This may be initially more difficult in this section. Suggestions:

- Jesus set out with his disciples on this journey to Jerusalem (9:51), and now he has arrived to meet his personal destiny. For him it is a momentous occasion, and he is personally filled with joy that it has come, and rejoices that disciples momentarily share his appreciation of the occasion – if they remained silent, the stones would cry out! How glad we are of his courage and selflessness. How he helps us to face our personal crises with courage. We are in his company and care, disciples carrying our own crosses after him.

- The two Jericho stories just before he reached Jerusalem show his intentions: the blind man (18:35-43), who followed him when he received his sight; and the Zacchaeus story (19:1-10) – the Son of Man has come to seek and save the lost. Jesus has come to Jerusalem to open eyes and heal the lostness of the human heart. He weeps at human refusal to accept his healing. Have we any doubt about his love and compassion for each of us, even in our most foolish times? He has come for us, to bring us salvation. Reflect for a moment on what that means to you, and what a difference it has made to your life.

3.4 *Challenge:* Consider the challenge to Jesus, to the disciples, and to ourselves.
- The challenge to Jesus is obvious. We admire his courage in coming to Jerusalem, though he foresees his fate; and his self-lessness. He makes a quite deliberate public statement for his disciples about his mission, in full knowledge of how the Jewish leadership and the Roman authorities may react to it. The statement implies that this is God's mission and nothing can stop it (he and his disciples will have a different under-standing of what that means). He weeps for the fate of the people of Jerusalem more than for his own fate, and charges them only with not recognising the moment, rather than with malice. He goes immediately to the temple, his Father's house (Luke 2:49), which he could not bear to leave as a boy, listening to the teachers of the Law, and purifies it (Mal 3:1-4: 'and the Lord whom you seek will suddenly come to his tem-ple'). Then he becomes the temple teacher of the message of salvation (in chapters 20-21 we find him daily in the temple teaching, as opposition from the leaders of the people grows). Pause for a moment to admire the picture of Jesus courageously intent upon the work of our salvation. Here is the Messiah-King, but Servant-King, facing the consequences of his decisions to follow the path set out by his Father.

- Luke has emphasised that disciples followed Jesus to Jerusalem, as he tried to teach them. What does Luke think the disciple Theophilus should learn here? Our journey through life is full of the joy and sorrow that emerge from this coming to Jerusalem. We are challenged to show courage, loyalty to Jesus, have a listening ear for the Master's words, have compassion for others even when they are against us, face our own 'exodus', our going to the Father along with Jesus. Above all, we appreciate the goodness and the rightness of what Jesus is doing, and know that the place to be is with him, fearful though we be. Pause for a moment to renew your commitment to Jesus.

- Later in the New Testament Jerusalem becomes a symbol for the church, and then for the final stage of God's kingdom, the heavenly Jerusalem. Thinking of Jerusalem as a symbol for the church, look again at vv 41-44, Jesus weeping over Jerusalem. Jesus is always facing his passion in his body, the church, with all the suffering of his brothers and sisters. He still weeps over the church, because of the lack of response from those who should be listening and fail to do so. But the church is us, and we are challenged to bear witness to Jesus by our faithful discipleship. Thank God for the church that has welcomed Jesus, spread the news of his saving grace throughout the world and proclaims him as 'the king who comes in the name of the Lord', though we are weak and sinful.

4. RESPONSE

There is much here to prompt a personal response of prayer. As a disciple of Jesus, put yourself among the crowd coming down the Mount of Olives into the city of Jerusalem to celebrate the Passover, the great commemoration of God's saving mercy for his people in the exodus from Egypt. We know there is a new exodus coming, for Jesus and for us, a new and more wonderful saving act of God for his people. So we praise God and salute Jesus in our own words, words of thanksgiving, loyalty, joy for the blessings of salvation, sorrow at the sin of the world, and the wounds of the pilgrim church, the missed opportunities, pleading for those heedlessly plunged into war and destruction by the pride and greed of others. We acknowledge our weakness and disloyalty to Jesus in times when we should be stronger. We ask for the gift of prayerfulness, which will sustain us in time of crisis. Too often we rely on our own strength: renew determination to pray 'not to be put to the test'.

5. CONTEMPLATION

Cultivate the mind of a pilgrim, following Jesus with hope, knowing weakness and failure, but holding on to him, and trusting in the immense love of our Father for us. Love the church, the new Jerusalem, as Jesus loved the Jerusalem of his day, though he wept for its foolishness and narrowness and missed opportunities. In spite of the pitfalls for individual and church, it is a joyful journey, an inspirational journey, to follow the footsteps of the Lord, so let your joy be seen!

Pick a text to live with, that you repeat regularly to yourself, which will remind you of Jesus coming to Jerusalem. 'Blessed is the king who comes in the name of the Lord'; 'My house shall be a house of prayer'; 'All the people were spellbound by what they heard.'

Prayer:

God our Father, we thank you with all our hearts for calling us to follow your Son, Jesus our Saviour. Help us to learn from his example of courage and obedience to your will; help us to meet with dignity and perseverance the trials and crosses in our lives; above all, help us to be truly joyful with the fullness of the new life he has won for us, and filled with the gifts of the Holy Spirit. We ask this through Christ our Lord. Amen.

SECTION C: THE JOURNEY TO THE FATHER

Session 15: The Last Supper (Luke 22:14-34)

1. FOCUS
Take time to focus the mind and heart on the presence of the Lord. For suggestions, see Introduction p 18 or Session 1 p 26.

Prayer:

> Lord Jesus, you embraced with joy the whole history of your people in celebrating the Passover meal with your disciples. You looked forward with joy to your own Passover to the Father, and left us a memorial of that Passover, giving new meaning to the bread and wine of the Passover meal. Help us to grow in understanding and love of the wonderful mystery of the Eucharist; may we always share this gift with joy, and find in it the strength to overcome our weakness and follow you with courage. Amen.

2. FAMILIARISATION
Read the text a few times until you become familiar with it. Jesus celebrates the Passover, gives it a new meaning. Then the other sections focus on the reactions of the disciples, and Jesus' words to them. Get the sequence in Luke clear in your mind; close your eyes and tell it over to yourself.

The Passover Meal

> 22:14 When the hour came, he took his place at the table,
> and the apostles with him.
> 15 He said to them,
> 'I have eagerly desired to eat this Passover with you
> before I suffer;
> 16 for I tell you, I will not eat it [again]
> until it is fulfilled in the kingdom of God.'
> 17 Then he took a cup, and after giving thanks, he said,
> 'Take this and divide it among yourselves;
> 18 for I tell you that from now on
> I will not drink of the fruit of the vine
> until the kingdom of God comes.'

Blessing of bread and wine, reinterpreted by Jesus.
19 Then he took a loaf of bread,
and when he had given thanks, he broke it
and gave it to them, saying,
'This is my body, which is given for you.
Do this in remembrance of me.'
20 And he did the same with the cup after supper, saying,
'This cup that is poured out for you
is the new covenant in my blood.'

Betrayal
21 'But see, the one who betrays me is with me,
for his hand is on the table.
22 For the Son of Man is going as it has been determined,
but woe to that one by whom he is betrayed.'
23 Then they began to ask one another,
which one of them it could be, who would do this.

Greatness in the Kingdom
24 A dispute also arose among them as to which one of them
was to be regarded as the greatest.
25 But he said to them,
'The kings of the Gentiles lord it over them;
and those in authority over them are called benefactors.
26 But not so with you; rather the greatest among you
must become like the youngest;
and the leader like one who serves.
27 For who is the greater,
the one who is at the table or the one who serves?
Is it not the one at the table?
But I am among you as one who serves. (*cf Mark 10:45*)
28 You are those who have stood by me in my trials;
29 and I confer on you,
just as my Father has conferred on me, a kingdom,
30 so that you may eat and drink at my table in my kingdom,
and you will sit on thrones judging the twelve tribes of Israel.

Simon Peter, strength and weakness
31 'Simon, Simon, listen!
Satan has demanded to sift all of you like wheat,
32 but I have prayed for you that your own faith may not fail;

and you, when once you have turned back,
strengthen your brothers.'
33 And he said to him, 'Lord, I am ready to go with you
to prison and to death!'
34 Jesus said, 'I tell you, Peter, the cock will not crow this day,
until you have denied three times that you know me.'

2.1 Background
Group leaders are urged to become familiar with the background before leading a group session; others are encouraged to read the text above and the background before coming to a group session. Reread the text in the light of the background information.

2.1.1 Luke gives a clear narrative of the celebration of the Passover meal (vv 15-18), followed by a reinterpretation of the blessing of the bread (before the meal), and of the 'cup after supper' (vv 19-20). Luke's text of the words of institution has differences from Mark/Matthew, but similarities to that of Paul in 1 Corinthians 11:23-26 ('my body that is for you, do this in remembrance of me'). There is a 'shorter text' of Luke in some manuscripts which omits the second part of v 19 and all of v 20, but the 'long text' is now almost universally accepted as the correct one (the omission possibly arose due to confusion about the 2 cups, v 17 and v 20).

2.1.2 *The first century Passover Meal* had 4 stages, and Luke's account of the Last Supper fits into Stage 1, the Preliminary Cup of wine (Luke 22:17), and Stage 3, where at the beginning of the meal proper the Father of the household said the blessing over the bread (Luke 22:19), and at the end of which comes Cup 3, the cup of blessing (Luke 22:20).

(1) Preliminary: A blessing (*qiddush*) of the feast. Cup 1 of wine *(corresponding to v 17 'Then he took a cup …')* Preliminary dish of herbs.
(2) Passover Liturgy: The Father recited the Passover story, answering the question of the youngest present: 'Why is this night different?' Singing of first part of Hallel (Praising) Psalms (113-114). Drinking of Cup 2.
(3) The meal proper: Blessing over unleavened bread (*massoth*), 'the bread of affliction'. *(v 19 'Then he took a loaf of bread …)*

Passover lamb eaten with *massoth* and bitter herbs. Cup 3 'the cup of blessing' *(v 20 'the cup after supper')*.

(4) Conclusion: Singing of second part of the Hallel Psalms (115-118).

It seems clear that the words of Jesus over the bread and wine in our Eucharist come from the blessing over the bread at the beginning of the meal proper, and Cup 3, the 'cup after supper'. Jesus takes these two rituals at the beginning and end of the meal, and gives them a new meaning. (For further information on this background, see Raymond Moloney SJ, *Our Splendid Eucharist*, Veritas, 2003, pp 33ff.)

2.1.3 The order of events at the Supper is Luke's own. Luke places together a number of disparate incidents which originally are unlikely to have taken place in this sequence. In doing so he produces a complex but highly instructive picture of Jesus and his disciples. He places the reference to betrayal by one of the twelve after the institution of the Eucharist (before in Mark/Matthew); follows it by the dispute about which of the disciples is the greatest (Mark/Matthew have this earlier at the second passion prophecy). Luke omits the difficult reference to 'give his life as a ransom for many' (Mk 10:45), based on the Great Servant Song (Isaiah 53:10-11; the exact meaning of the text is difficult), and contents himself with a more general reference to the Servant of God in Isaiah, 'I am among you as one who serves' (v 27). He adds the saying of Jesus about giving a share in his kingdom to the apostles (Matthew has this at 19:28); then a saying of Jesus about the sifting by Satan of Peter and the others (prepared for at 4:13 and 22:3, 'Satan entered into Judas'); and a special role is given to Peter (given in Matthew 16:18ff. and John 21:15ff.) He is to strengthen the others after his own conversion. Peter's protestation of loyalty and the prophecy of his denial come at the Supper (in Mark/Matthew they come on the way to Gethsemane).

Luke therefore deliberately sets up a contrast between Jesus the servant who is to give himself for his disciples, and the disciples who worry about which of them is the greatest. He contrasts the generosity of Jesus, who gives them both the Eucharistic bread and wine and the gift of a share in his kingdom including the invitation to eat and drink at his table in his kingdom, with the disciples' weakness that leads to betrayal and the denial of Jesus in the face of Satan's sifting. All the future glories and woes of the church are there, the magnificent gifts and invitations, but the concern for status and power rather than service, the betrayals and denials. In spite of every betrayal, Jesus remains compassionate towards the disciples, prays for Peter, and gives hope that he will be converted and able to strengthen his brethren. This prepares for the scene of the agony, where the disciples fail to 'pray not to be put to the test' before the passion, and therefore are in danger of falling away.

2.1.4 Interpretation of Calvary. The Last Supper interprets for us the events to come on Calvary. The bread broken and given to be consumed becomes an effective symbol of his body broken and 'given for you' on the cross. Only Luke has on Calvary the words of Jesus, 'Father into your hands I commend [give] my spirit' (23:46). The 'cup after supper' takes on a new meaning, 'poured out for you', 'the new covenant in my blood'. So the wine poured out to be consumed anticipates the blood of Jesus poured out for his people on Calvary, an oblation of himself that brings a new covenant relationship between his disciples and God. By an 'effective symbol' we mean a symbol which actually contains what it represents: 'This is my body', 'This cup ... is the new covenant in my blood'.

3. REFLECTION

Take a period of quiet to digest the text. You may prefer to concentrate on one portion of it at this time. Group leaders may wish to invite those who feel comfortable to share briefly what initially strikes them about the text.

3.1 Journey: The Last Supper is a resting point on the journey, a time of celebrating together, restoration and strengthening for what is to come. Jesus embraces the history of his people, celebrates the first exodus, gives it a new meaning, and prepares himself and his disciples for the remainder of the journey, his exodus to the Father. Here we have a preview of the journey (exodus) to come, and look back briefly to the first Passover, the exodus from Egypt. The concerns of the disciples show how ill prepared they still are to accompany Jesus on the last stages of the journey to Calvary and beyond. Note Jesus' eagerness to eat this Passover and how he looks forward to its fulfilment, his own Passover to the Father. The disciples were far from ready to share his eagerness. How do you feel about Jesus' desire to carry out his mission in spite of all that was to come? How do you feel about your own readiness to follow him on the journey that leads to God our Father? Reflect on the Eucharist as 'food for the journey' (*viaticum*), strengthening us to follow in the footsteps of Jesus. He could not say more clearly: 'I will be with you; do not be afraid.'

3.2 Joy: Note again Jesus' eager desire to eat this Passover meal with his disciples, and his certainty that it will be fulfilled in the kingdom of God, that they will all meet again at the banquet in the kingdom. We can see how we must be joyful because of the gift of the Eucharist, but at first the rest of the scene seems depressing. It is all about power-seeking and betrayal. It makes me conscious of my own weakness, and my failure to allow the gift of Jesus to change me. But look again. In spite of his realistic understanding of the disciples' weakness, Jesus maintains a compassion for them, a serenity, a supportive love that is impressive and gives me hope. He is among them as one who serves (v 27); he thanks them for standing by him in his trials (v 28); he gives them a share in his kingdom. They will 'eat and drink at [his] table in [his] kingdom' (v 30), they will have power to judge 'the twelve tribes of Israel', presumably the Christian community, the reconstituted Israel (v 30). He knows that Simon Peter will betray him, but he has prayed for him and is confident of his conversion ('when – *not if* – you have turned back'), and trusts Simon to strengthen the others. All this, I think, should give us great sources of joy. We of course rejoice in the gift of the Eucharist, the self-giving of Jesus which makes him so desire, and at what cost, to be close to us, to live within us. But a great source of joy and consolation to me is the perception that every time I celebrate the Eucharist, and like the disciples, so soon after show all my failings and weaknesses and never seem to learn, yet still, Jesus is there with reassurance and prayer for me, and even gratitude to me for sticking with him, healing me with his compassion and love. How do you feel about that? Does it send you back to the Eucharist with hope? Does it give you a better understanding of how Jesus sees the good in you, and is full of healing compassion for your weaknesses?

3.3 *Personal:* By 'personal' we mean the closeness of Jesus to his Father, and his closeness to the disciples. Luke skilfully paints an intimate picture of Jesus' desire to complete his journey to the Father, his embracing of the Father's will, and his desire to give himself to the Father, and to give himself to his disciples in the Eucharist. In spite of the realism of the picture of the disciples' humanness, Jesus is gentle, has high expectations for them, is compassionate towards them, as we have noted above.

Put yourself in the disciples' place. Allow yourself to accept the intimacy of Jesus handing to you the bread and wine which are statements of his great love for you: 'My body which is given for you', 'This cup that is poured out for you.' Jesus is the servant: 'I am among you as one who serves.' He gives us a share in his own future kingship (his vocation to serve). He is grateful for our loyalty to him, in spite of our possible lack of courage. He prays for us, as he prays for Simon, that we may be converted and may be strong enough in whatever way we can to help our brothers and sisters. How do you feel about this? Does it make you feel inadequate, or build you up? Does it bring Jesus closer to you? Do you feel his hopes for you?

We are ready enough to identify with the disciples' weaknesses, and the danger of being sifted by Satan in time of crisis. We know our mixture of loyalty to Jesus and our desire for status, our jealousy of others. But let us also know Jesus' love and compassion, and his delight in our small attempts to serve him faithfully. Let him nourish us with his special gift of himself in the Eucharist.

3.4 *Challenge:* Jesus gives us the Eucharist: it points to his self-giving on the cross. When he says, 'Do this in remembrance of me', he challenges us both to repeat this sacred rite in his memory, and to be this kind of disciple, self-giving like Jesus, one who serves. It is a tough challenge. We have the Eucharist to nourish and strengthen us, to mould us into the image of Jesus. We know that we must then *live* the Eucharist in our lives. We see clearly laid out before us by Luke how little real difference that Eucharist initially made in the disciples' attitudes and behaviour. We know that it is often just so with us. Jesus challenges us to change, to allow the Eucharist to make us different, so we can be self-giving like him, able to serve. The beginning of change may be the acceptance of ourselves and others with all our weaknesses, and trust not in ourselves, but in his forgiveness and his prayer for our conversion ('turning round'). He challenges us to strengthen others if we can, to be loyal and to keep close to him in times of crisis and danger. The reality of Satan who can sift us like wheat means we have to be close to Jesus and to the Father in prayer. If it seems beyond our strength, remember his healing and compassionate presence, his gratitude for our small attempts to be loyal disciples.

4. RESPONSE

We need a period of quiet after our reflections to respond to the passage and to the Lord in prayer. We quietly give thanks for the gift of the Eucharist. We ask help to celebrate it well, and to try to live it in our daily lives. What changes do you need to make to do better? Seek the help of the Holy Spirit. We may deplore our failures, admit our weakness in the face of temptation, be conscious of rivalries and petty jealousies. So we ask for healing, for prayerfulness, for a spirit of service and cooperation. Trust in his goodness; he gives himself 'for us', and appreciates our efforts at fidelity. Assure him of our loyalty, knowing that like Peter, we may let him down. But with his help we will one day, please God, eat and drink at his table in heaven.

If you wish, try this exercise. Identify with the bread that Jesus takes: ask Jesus to take you, poor bread, in his hands, to be changed; with him give thanks and blessing to God for the gift of yourself, pray that you may be able to allow yourself to be broken like the bread in his service, that you will accept all the bruises of life that break you, and allow yourself to be given to God, to Jesus, to your brothers and sisters. Bread that is broken, given and consumed is the symbol of Jesus given for us. Lord, help us to become more like you.

5. CONTEMPLATION

The Eucharistic Celebration is a sacred event. Sometimes events pass too quickly for us to appreciate or respond to all that is happening. So we need to have a eucharistic mentality, whereby we contemplate Jesus' giving of himself for us to the Father, and to us in the sacrament. Our presence with the Blessed Eucharist allows us to deepen our understanding of Jesus the Giver, who calls us to give ourselves. We offer ourselves with him to God our Father, but our offering is so tentative and conditioned by our weakness and hesitations that it needs to be repeated often. Keep the Last Supper in your mind: select a text to repeat often, to help your remembering. 'This is my body, which is given for you'; 'The new covenant in my blood'; 'I am among you as one who serves.'

Prayer:

O sacred banquet, in which Christ is received, the memory of his passion is recalled, the mind is filled with grace, and a pledge of future glory is given to us! Amen.

Session 16: Agony in the Garden (Luke 22:39-46)

1. FOCUS

Take time to focus the mind and heart on the presence of the Lord. For suggestions see Introduction p 18 or Session 1 p 26.

Prayer:

> Lord, you turned to your Father in earnest prayer before your passion, to find the strength in your humanity to face the cruelty of your enemies, the power of darkness, the weakness of your friends. Lord, teach us to pray that we may not be tested beyond our strength or readiness, for like the apostles, we often fall asleep to our real needs and our perils. Let us not betray you in our weakness, and may your healing touch restore and renew us. Amen.

2. FAMILIARISATION

Spend some time quietly getting to know the Lucan text. It is set out below with an introduction (v 39), followed by a chiastic pattern (see 2.1.2), used to highlight ideas placed in the prominent positions – the central (v 42) and final places (v 46). Note how A and A1 are similar, B and B1 likewise. Verses 43-44 are in italics, indicating that they are missing in many manuscripts, and not certainly by Luke's hand, though still inspired scripture. These verses do not fit the pattern that seems to be present in the other verses. Try to see the pattern, and focus on the big ideas in v 42 and v 46 – the prayer of Jesus, and his advice to the disciples.

Introduction

> 22.39 He came out and went, as was his custom,
> to the Mount of Olives; and the disciples followed him.

The prayer of Jesus

> 40 When he reached the place, he said to them,
> *'Pray that you may not come into the time of trial.'* [A]
> 41 Then he withdrew from them about a stone's throw, [B]
> knelt down, and prayed,
> 42 'Father, if you are willing, remove this cup from me; [C]
> yet, *not my will but yours be done.'*

142

43 [Then an angel from heaven appeared to him
and gave him strength.
44 In his anguish he prayed more earnestly,
and his sweat became like great drops of blood
falling down on the ground.]
45 When he got up from prayer, [B1]
he came to the disciples
and found them sleeping because of grief,
46 and he said to them, 'Why are you sleeping?
Get up and *pray that you may not come into the time of trial.'* [A1]

2.1 Background

Study of this material should be part of a leader's preparation for a group session; other group members are urged to spend time with the text and the background notes before coming to the group meeting. It is recommended to reread the text in the light of the background information.

2.1.1 Luke's Editing: Luke's account of the agony in the garden has been given his own treatment and emphasis. Jesus is the exemplar of earnest prayer to God our Father in time of need, and in line with Luke's preference for showing the Master in serene and loving acceptance of the Father's will, he plays down the suffering of Jesus – except strangely in the famous v 44, 'His sweat became like great drops of blood falling down to the ground.' Many manuscripts omit vv 43-44 from the text, and they do not fit readily with the structure of the text (see 2.1.2), nor with the usual preference of Luke. Many reliable scholars believe that these verses were not originally written by Luke, though that does not prevent their being inspired scripture and worthy of our prayerful reflection.

2.1.2 Structure: An example of what is called *chiastic structure* may be seen in vv 40-46 (without vv 43-44). In this structure, similar ideas or phrases are set out in a concentric pattern (A B C B A), usually with special stress on the central idea, and secondary stress on the final one. Luke uses this pattern to emphasise the supreme importance of prayer before critical events, in order to find acceptance of the Father's will and to seek the Father's strength to face the ordeal. In 40 (A) and 46 (A1) Jesus begs his disciples to pray not to come into the time of trial. The advice is not heeded by sleepy disciples –'sleeping because of grief'. Note that Luke does not single out Peter, James and John; so Jesus' words are addressed to all the disciples (so indirectly to all of us). In 41 (B) Jesus withdraws from them to pray, in 45 (B1) he returns to the disciples after prayer. V 42 (C) is central and therefore intended to give emphasis to Jesus' prayer to the Father and acceptance of the Father's will. This is contrasted with the disciples' failure to pray in a time of great peril, where their very salvation is in crisis. Therefore they show weakness when the passion begins. The message is obvious: we must pray not to be put to the test. Though the disciples are weak, Luke has great respect for the friends of Jesus, and suggests that they were 'sleeping because of grief', sorrow for the coming fate of their Master; and he simply does not mention that they all fled when Jesus was arrested.

2.1.3 The Insertion: Though possibly inserted later (either by Luke or another hand), vv 43-44 help us to realise that the decision to accept the Father's will was not matter of fact, but a deep personal struggle for the human Jesus, whose humanity shrank from the humiliation and afflictions to come. 'An angel from heaven' gave him strength, showing that God our Father consoles and strengthens us in time of trial. The sequence is a little strange, the angel's strengthening of him being followed by his more anguished prayer and his sweat 'becoming like (*hosai*, as it were?) great drops of blood falling to the ground'. This verse is hard to reconcile with Luke's picture of Jesus, whom he presents as serene and obedient in the face of his coming suffering. It is probably important to note that the text does not say that his sweat became drops of blood, but 'became *like* great drops of blood' – an attempt to express terrible agony using imaginative language rather than a literal description of what happened.

2.1.4 God's Will: It is easy, but very unwise, to get drawn into an outmoded theology of an angry God demanding the blood of his Son to save sinful humanity. It is too big a subject to deal with here. For the sake of the group leader who may have to field difficult questions, three things need to be said. Firstly, we know that the sending of the Beloved Son, and the whole process of salvation, is prompted by the Father's love for his people. John 3:16 says: 'For God so loved the world that he gave his only Son, so that anyone who believes in him may not perish, but may have eternal life.' So Jesus does not have to placate an angry Father; he does what he does because the Father loves us and wishes us to be saved. Secondly, it is primarily by the love and obedience of Jesus that we are saved, admittedly made visible in and through his physical and mental suffering. As we move further away from the original events, the evangelists Luke and John tend to understate the physical sufferings of Jesus to concentrate on the meaning and purpose behind them. Contrast the close relationship between Jesus and the Father in the Lucan crucifixion scene – see Session 18 – with the cry of Jesus on the cross in Mark/Matthew, 'My God, my God, why have you forsaken me?'(Mark 15:34, Matthew 27:46, omitted by Luke). Thirdly, there is an alternative theory, worth exploring, that God did not demand the death of his Son, but did demand that he continue his mission in a loving way; and fidelity to his mission inevitably led to his death because of the sinful cruelty of human beings and the enmity of Satan. This raises the distinction between what God *allows* to happen, his *permissive* will, and what God *wants* to happen, his *positive* will. The positive will of God is that Jesus should faithfully carry out his mission of love; the permissive will of God is to refuse to intervene to prevent the suffering which resulted from fidelity to his mission.

3. REFLECTION

Take a period of quiet to digest the text. Leaders may wish to allow or encourage participants who feel comfortable with it to share their initial feelings about the text.

3.1 Journey: Reflect upon great turning points in life, where we move, often painfully, from one stage of life to another. The Greeks have a word for it, *kairos*, the critical time, which may also be a time of opportunity. The prayer in the garden was obviously a great turning point in the life of Jesus, when he embraced his destiny with trepidation, but with courage and obedience to the will of the Father. It was a crisis for the disciples also, where they failed to act on the repeated advice of Jesus.

Great turning points in our lives require prayer and courage, dependence on God rather than on our own resources. Sometimes young people with the world at their feet find this a bit unreal; older people probably already know the reality of sickness, emotional conflicts, hints of mortality, the inevitability of death. People say with brave understatement, 'You have to keep going.' Young people too are now in great need of spiritual resources to face the demands of growing up, educational challenges, demanding relationships, disappointments, rejection, and in far too many cases are unable to continue the struggle and take their own lives. We are in tremendous need of prayer, and of confidence in God's strengthening presence, prayer for ourselves and for each other, especially the young and the elderly. Jesus gives us example and encouragement, and is always forgiving if we fail. In time of failure or bereavement it can be very hard to accept 'God's will' (see 2.1.4), which can be perceived as harsh and cruel, leading us to be angry and push God away when we need him most. If we have listened to Jesus asking us to take up our cross and follow him (Session 8), we know (at least with our heads) that difficulties, trials, crises are a normal part of life, that they can be destructive but also life-giving, and that God gives strength and courage if we turn to him in prayer.

3.2 *Joy:* You may skip this Key if you think that here is definitely not the place for it! We certainly have to think of joy in a deeper but real sense, the peace and inner strength that Jesus found in his prayer and acceptance. Have you seen the serenity and peace of some people in the face of suffering or death? It can be really impressive. It is not achieved without much prayer and faith, but that is what Jesus urges upon his disciples, then and now.

3.3 *Personal:* Luke again stresses the need for a close personal relationship with God. Jesus prays, 'Father, if you are willing ... yet, not my will but yours be done.' Jesus does not come to acceptance with a statement; the statement sums up his life and his long and intense prayer. Similarly, disciples need a close personal relationship with Jesus. When Jesus came to the Mount of Olives, 'the disciples followed him'. The following will be critical for them, for their future and their salvation. Their personal relationship to Jesus and to God the Father is at crisis point. Jesus shows his concern for them in his repeated plea that they need to pray for strength. He himself prays earnestly for the cup to pass, but only if it is the Father's will. Following Jesus at this stage of his mission is difficult, and disciples will simply fail if they rely on their own strength. Luke makes allowance, as is his wont, for the disciples. Jesus found them 'sleeping because of grief'. We have critical times in our lives when we face decisions, temptations, illness, bereavement, grief, all of which may lead to a strengthened relationship to Jesus, or the loss of that relationship. Do you feel there were times when you were strengthened and grew closer to God as a result of a crisis in your life? Do you remember times when your relationship to God was under severe strain? The commitment of faith that a disciple must make is that of Peter in John 6:68, 'Lord, to whom can we go? You have the words of eternal life.' Jesus says prayer, trust, loyalty, love will get us through, and he personally knows that it can be a tough struggle. (The inserted verses 43-44 help us to know that Jesus' decision to accept the Father's will was not matter of fact, but a deep personal struggle that was prolonged and draining for Jesus, but that led to peace.) But he forgives our stumbling attempts to follow him.

3.4 Challenge: Reflection on this scene brings us to understand Jesus' words, 'If any want to become my followers, let them deny themselves and take up their cross daily and follow me' (9:23). Our challenge is to pray for strength to follow in hard times as well as in joyful, to be realistic about our own weakness, and to rely on God. Our consolation is that help will be given: Jesus is concerned for us, and has said, 'Ask, and it will be given you' (11:9). What may not be given is escape from the difficulties ahead, but strength to face them will be given: 'the heavenly Father [will] give the Holy Spirit to those who ask him' (11:13).

4. RESPONSE

A prayerful response to the Agony may have to be very private, and may depend on one's current circumstances. A personal and very honest response is the best one. One or more of the following suggestions may be useful as an initial stimulus.

A traditional way of praying about the Agony is to try to

imagine the pain and mental anguish of Jesus and do our best to empathise with him. Verses 43 and 44 help here. Luke, however, seems to want us to focus on Jesus' love and acceptance of his Father's will, and his example of prayer.

So the *first response* might be thanksgiving, gratitude to Jesus for his love and willingness to accept the cross for us. As his body is racked with grief and foreboding, we remember his words, 'This is my body, given for you' (22:19).

A second response might be offering to him and with him all your bodily and mental ills: 'This is my body given for you, Lord, and in union with you.' Give some time to this idea.

Thirdly, we may recall our mistakes and failures in times of crisis, and understand our failure to pray, our foolish reliance on our own powers. Ask for forgiveness, for the gift of wisdom. *Jesus, help me to know my need of prayer, my need of God's help and strength in the face of difficult decisions and trials.*

Fourthly, resolve not to be too disturbed about past failures, relying on Jesus' compassion and his intercession for us. He looks upon us with love when we fail, as he did on Peter. 'The Lord turned and looked at Peter' (22:61). He came to heal our failures and our weakness, and we need to allow his healing compassion to penetrate our outward shell and fill our hearts. *Look upon us, Lord, and open us up to your healing mercy.*

Fifthly, we need to leave this prayer with a renewed sense of personal attachment to Jesus, and through him with God our Father. Within that relationship, failures are healed and forgiven. Without that, failures leave us isolated, ashamed and dispirited – literally, without the Spirit of God in us. *Lord, I am your disciple; I wish to follow you in good times and bad; help me to be true to my covenant commitment with you.*

5. CONTEMPLATION

Jesus in this critical time is a wise, courageous, determined and compassionate leader. I want to keep that picture of him in my mind. And I want to foster within myself a sense of trust in God's strengthening love. 'Do not be afraid, I will be with you' is God's constant message to willing but weak disciples. Nothing comes easily, but nothing is impossible with God. I belong to him, body, soul and spirit. My text to ponder is 'Not my will but yours be done', or 'Pray that you may not come into the time of trial.'

Prayer:

Lord, we give you heartfelt thanks for your love and accept-ance of the cross for us, and we ask you to help us in our faltering steps to follow your way. Teach us to pray. Teach us acceptance of life's trials and conflicts, and help us to put our trust in your strengthening presence, come what may. Give us the gifts of your Spirit that we may have courage and wis-dom. Amen

Restore us, O God; let your face shine, that we may be saved. *(Psalm 80:3; cf vv 7, 19)*

The Lord bless you and keep you:
the Lord make his face to shine upon you,
and be gracious to you.
The Lord lift up his countenance upon you,
and give you peace.
(Numbers 6:24-26)

Session 17: Jesus before the Council (Luke 22:54–23:1)

1. FOCUS

Take time to focus the mind and heart on the presence of the Lord. For suggestions see Introduction p 18 or Session 1 p 26.

Prayer:

> Lord, Luke can hardly bear the thought of you being put on trial, but he admires your courage and your words of testimony. Help us to listen to your words, help us to be courageous when our faith is challenged, and help us to bear witness to you by the lives we lead. Amen.

2. FAMILIARISATION

Take time to become familiar with the text. After Jesus' arrest, he is taken to the high priest's house; Peter follows, when challenged denies knowing him, but weeps when Jesus catches his eye. Jesus is mocked, kept overnight, and in the morning brought before the Council of the Jews. There is more of a testimony than a trial, and then they bring him to Pilate, the Roman governor.

Jesus taken into custody

> 22:54 Then they seized him and led him away,
> bringing him into the high priest's house.

Peter's denials and conversion

> But Peter was following at a distance.
> 55 When they had kindled a fire in the midst of the courtyard and sat down together, Peter sat among them.
> 56 Then a servant-girl, seeing him in the firelight,
> stared at him and said, 'This man also was with him.'
> 57 But he denied it, saying, 'Woman, I do not know him.'
> 58 A little later someone else, on seeing him, said,
> 'You also are one of them.' But Peter said, 'Man, I am not!'
> 59 But about an hour later, still another kept insisting,
> 'Surely this man also was with him; for he is a Galilean.'
> 60 But Peter said,
> 'Man, I do not know what you are talking about!'
> At that moment, while he was still speaking,
> the cock crowed.

61 The Lord turned and looked at Peter.
Then Peter remembered the word of the Lord,
how he had said to him,
'Before the cock crows today, you will deny me three times.'
62 And he went out and wept bitterly.

Mockery from the captors
63 Now the men who were holding him
began to mock him and beat him;
64 they also blindfolded him and kept asking him,
'Prophesy! Who is it that struck you?'
65 They kept heaping many other insults on him.

Jesus' testimony before the Council
66 When day came, the assembly of the elders of the people,
both chief priests and scribes, gathered together,
and they brought him to their council.
67 They said, 'If you are the Messiah, tell us.'
He replied, 'If I tell you, you will not believe;
68 and if I question you, you will not answer.
69 But from now on the Son of Man
will be seated at the right hand of the power of God.'
70 All of them asked, 'Are you, then, the Son of God?'
He said to them, 'You say that I am.'
71 Then they said, 'What further testimony do we need?
We have heard it ourselves from his own lips!'
23:1 Then the assembly rose as a body
and brought Jesus before Pilate.

2.1 Background
The background information is a little bit complex, but it will help if you persevere! Leaders as always should make themselves familiar with the background before leading a session. All who attend group sessions should read the text and the background notes before attending the group meeting. It helps to reread the text in the light of the background information.

2.1.1 Three distinct episodes are included in Luke's narrative about Jesus being held in custody by the Jewish authorities: Peter's triple denial (vv 55-62), mockery of Jesus by those who held him captive, possibly the temple guard, already prophesied by Jesus (18:32: 'he will be mocked and insulted'), vv 63-65; and the interrogation of Jesus before the Council (hardly a trial), vv 66-71.

2.1.2 The sequence of events during the trials of Jesus is difficult to reconstruct, as the gospels do not give the same sequence, and Luke differs from his main source, Mark. The following table of events in Mark/Matthew, Luke and John may help us to draw some conclusions. Consult, if you wish, Mark 14:53–15:1; Matthew 26:57–27:2; John 18:12-28.

Time	Mark/Matthew	Luke	John
Night	Peter follows Jesus Trial before the High Priest (Mt names Caiaphas) Maltreatment Peter's denials	Peter follows Jesus Peter's denials Mockery of Jesus	Peter's first denial Interrogation before Annas Peter's 2nd and 3rd denials
Morning	Trial (no content)	Trial/ interrogation Edited content of Mk/Mt night trial	Jesus sent to Caiaphas but no trial is recounted

Mark and Matthew have a full meeting of the Sanhedrin by night, presided over by the High Priest (unnamed by Mark, named as Caiaphas by Matthew). Luke has no night trial, John had an informal interrogation before Annas (High Priest 6-15 AD, deposed by the Romans, but still considered by many as the rightful high priest, father-in-law of Caiaphas). A full meeting of the Sanhedrin by night seems unlikely and of doubtful legality. A plausible sequence of events is that there was an interrogation of Jesus during the night he was arrested, probably before

Annas (Matthew put in the name of the 'official' high priest Caiaphas); then he was sent to Caiaphas (officially appointed by the Romans 18-36 AD), and a formal trial took place in the morning before Caiaphas. Mark knew that Jesus was brought before the high priest when he was arrested, and he had information about a trial, so he put all he knew into the night session. Matthew followed Mark, adding the name of the 'official' high priest, Caiaphas. John has no morning trial for his own editorial reasons, and Luke, trying to preserve what he considers the more likely historical sequence, has put the trial in the morning, heavily editing the content of Mark's night trial. We will see below that Luke has his own reasons for editing the content as he did.

2.1.3 *Luke's editing:* what looks like a formal trial in Mark/Matthew, with the high priest presiding and interrogating Jesus, with witnesses, accusations and a verdict, becomes in Luke an occasion for Jesus to give testimony about his identity and future glory. Luke edits out the witnesses and the high priest (all the questions and responses come from the whole council, 'they said', 'all of them asked'). The only mention of blasphemy, of which Jesus is accused in Mark, comes with reference to the captor's ill-treatment of Jesus, v 65 (*lit.* 'they said many other things to him, blaspheming'). There is no verdict of guilty, and no sentence proposed; they simply agree to take him to Pilate, the Roman governor. When Jesus bears testimony to his identity and future dignity, they said, 'What further testimony do we need? We have heard it ourselves from his own lips!' They do not of course intend to accept Jesus' testimony as true, but Luke's wording of their answer is something that a Christian believer can wholeheartedly accept, that Jesus confirms from his own mouth that he is Messiah and Son of God.

2.1.4 *Peter's Denials:* Luke has some variations compared to the other gospels. The denials are all given together before the mockery and the interrogations. In the others gospels the interrogation comes in the middle of the narrative about Peter; John has the second and third denials after the interrogation. Luke has no night interrogation, so the 3 denials have to come first. Luke also tones down Peter's denials a little, out of respect for him; he does not curse and swear that he does not know Jesus as in Mark 14:71. Luke's characteristic addition is v 61, 'The Lord turned and looked at Peter. Then Peter remembered the word of the Lord ... and he went out and wept bitterly' (the last part shared by Matthew 26:75 and Mark 14:72). Here are two characteristic features of the Lucan narrative, that the conversion of Peter begins with the very personal meeting of eyes with Jesus, and that Jesus' prophecy is fulfilled (just before he is mocked as a prophet by his captors). Peter is seen as meeting his time of trial, but unprepared, being sifted by Satan. Jesus has prayed for him, and his conversion begins with the glance of Jesus.

2.1.5 The mockery of Jesus: The mockery is also toned down by Luke in comparison with Mark. Jesus has foretold in 18:32 that he would be mocked and insulted, sharing the fate of many prophets during the history of God's people. Jesus is hooded and threatened (methods of abuse do not change all that much over the centuries), and asked to prophesy only in mockery.

2.1.6 Jesus' testimony: When they ask if he is the Messiah (the Christ), Jesus evades a direct answer – he says they have already shown they are not prepared to have an honest dialogue with him. But he does make a striking testimony (close to Mark 14:62 / Matthew 26:64) which combines a reference to (i) Daniel 7:13f, 'As I watched in the night visions, I saw one like a human being, [Aramaic: like a son of man] coming with the clouds of heaven, and he came to the Ancient One ... (14) To him was given dominion and glory and kingship'; and (ii) Psalm 110:1 (LXX Ps 109), a royal text used at the coronation of kings of the line of David, which later took on a messianic meaning: 'The Lord (i.e. God) says to my lord (i.e. the king, in later interpretation, the messiah), Sit at my right hand.'

Luke's text reads: 'But from now on the Son of Man will be seated at the right hand of the power of God.' Compare Mark 14:62: 'I am [the Messiah], and you will see the Son of Man seated at the right hand of the Power, and coming with the clouds of heaven.' Luke omits 'I am', which he does not think Jesus would have said so bluntly under interrogation; omits also 'you will see'. Only believers, in his view, will see the Son in glory. He uses the phrase 'at the right hand of the power of God' as more intelligible to a gentile readership that Mark's personification of 'Power' as a title for God. He omits 'coming on the clouds of heaven' which weakens the reference to Daniel, but suits Luke's shift of emphasis from Mark's reference to the second coming in glory, to the time of his resurrection, the completion of Jesus' journey (exodus) to the Father. Therefore he adds 'from now on', i.e. after the resurrection believers will experience the power of the Son of Man. This is powerful testimony from the believer's point of view, and 'they', the members of the Sanhedrin, are ironically seen as bearing witness to the testimony of Jesus when they say, 'What further need have we of testimony; we have heard it ourselves from his own lips.'

2.1.7 Who is Jesus? Jesus is questioned about the two titles, Messiah and Son of God. Some commentators see these as being virtually equivalent, both messianic titles, but Luke's editing seems to distinguish them carefully by two distinct questions, so that 'Son of God' refers to his divine Sonship. To the prompt, 'If you are the Messiah, tell us', Jesus answers evasively, in contrast to Mark, perhaps because of the political entanglements surrounding the title. To the question, 'Are you then the Son of God', he answers, 'It is you who say that I am.' This answer does not deny it, but says it is their formulation, and that he might not agree to their understanding of the title. Luke has really edited this section for Christian believers, and intends them to accept that Jesus is the Messiah of the line of David, the Son of Man who will be given dominion by God, and more than that, the divine Son of God. These titles have already been given him by the angel in the annunciation story, Luke 1:32f (session 2): 'He will be great, and will be called Son of the Most High [Son of God], and the Lord will give to him the throne of his ancestor David [Messiah]. He will reign over the house of Jacob forever and of his kingdom there will be no end [Son of Man, as in Daniel]'.

3. Reflection
Now take a period of quiet to allow the Spirit to nourish your spirit, that your reflection may be fruitful. Leaders as ever may wish to begin discussion of the text by allowing volunteers to voice briefly what strikes them most forcibly in the narrative.

3.1 Journey: From now events move fast towards the completion of Jesus' exodus, his journey to the Father. Luke presents him as beginning the journey calmly and courageously, silent before his captors, except where testimony is needed for the truth to be defended. His words to the Council tell us of the goal of the journey, sitting 'at the right hand of the power of God'. We are assured of his triumph over Satan, and over all the suffering he must face. Peter attempts to 'follow', but from a distance (don't we all!). He is not prepared for the time of trial, and gives way to fear and cowardice. For all his willingness, he is too weak to stand up to challenges. How can Peter close that gap and find strength? Only when he looks at the face of Jesus, repents and learns to pray, so that he may rely on God and not on himself. What do you or I need to do to get closer to Jesus on his journey? To accept tranquilly that we go to the Father with him or not at all? What are the challenges, the questions that keep us back? Picture Jesus looking at you with his clear eyes, his calm power, his hope for you, his assurance of support and prayer. Do you see only reproach or disappointment in his eyes? Or does the picture that Luke paints not suggest that Jesus understands us, prays for us, holds out a hand to help us on the way, smiles in encouragement? Remind yourself about the meaning of exodus: we have to keep our eyes on the goal, where we are going, we have to remember that the Lord is with us, we have to expect difficulties on the way, we have to pray; the goal will be well worth it. So put your eyes again on the goal of Jesus' journey: 'from now on the Son of Man will be seated at the right hand of the power of God.' There he prays for us, as he prayed for Peter. Does this give you courage on your own journey, wherever you may be on the journey at this time?

3.2 Joy: Though Jesus is on trial, humiliated and mocked, Luke does his best to show us the positives in the situation. So look for the message of hope, the good news for you. In Peter's denials the good news is that Jesus looks on him with love even though Peter has denied him, and Peter begins his process of conversion. So he is going to get through, even strengthen others, in spite of his human weakness. Hope for us yet?

In the mockery of Jesus there isn't much joy, and Luke does

his best to turn his eyes away. He is mocked as a prophet, just as his prophecy that he would be mocked is being fulfilled. So we know that he really is the prophet of God, as he endures with silence the small-minded abuse of his guards.

The interrogation, as presented by Luke, is a passage to give us hope, for Luke uses it to present testimony about Jesus' identity and future glory. Jesus will be the judge, and he is the one even now giving the verdict to his questioners. 'From now on' – and we live in that period of the resurrection, the time of the church – 'the Son of Man will be seated at the right hand of the power of God.' We rejoice in his glory. Have you experienced his power? Do you feel that he prays for you to the Father, especially when you are in trouble?

3.3 Personal: From Peter's denials we have the perfect picture of how Luke sees Jesus with his disciples. It is the personal face to face meeting that brings Peter to the realisation of what he has done, and he weeps bitterly. But it is not a look of condemnation, but a look of love and belief in Peter that he may be saved. It was because of Jesus' prayer for him that Peter had the grace to change. Are you able to identify with Peter, now or at any time in your life? How close is your relationship with Jesus? We may grow hot and cold, but he is always there. Restore us, O God, let your face shine, that we may be saved (Ps 80:3).

Gazing at the mockery scene, we can be full of empathy for the Lord who is insulted. It is our privilege to offer him thanks and praise, and to try to make some reparation for the insults and indifference which he meets daily. Think of the insults and abuse Jesus receives in his Body, his brothers and sisters, the mockery offered to the weak, the neglected, the bullying, abuse of children, the racism, the hate and torture that Jesus still experiences in his 'little ones' with whom he identifies. We need to repent of any abuse in word or deed that we have offered, even in 'fun', to our brothers and sisters, his brothers and sisters. Do not be afraid when you are challenged and derided for your faith: he promises to be with you.

In the 'trial' scene, 'they' try to get Jesus to say who he is, so that they can find evidence to condemn him. But Luke presents Jesus giving testimony to his identity and future glory for believers. So ask yourself the question that he would like each of us to answer. 'Who do you say that I am?' Our passage uses the titles Messiah, Son of Man, Son of God. Tell Jesus in your own words who he is for you, and perhaps you would go on to call him friend, brother, saviour, teacher – or whatever expresses for you your personal relationship to him. Then think how he might address you!

3.4 Challenge: The oldest challenge is to be with Jesus and loyal to him when things are going badly for us, not just when all in the garden is rosy. The challenge is to know that if we follow Jesus, there will be hard times as well as lovely times. Learn from Peter that each of us needs to pray to be able to face the times of trial and temptation. We need to keep our eyes on the face of Jesus. Remembering all that he has been through for us helps us to re-alise that he knows what it is like to face hard times and hard decisions, and that he will be with us. We need a close relationship with him, one that touches our hearts and emotions, not just our heads. We need to avoid, or at least be aware of, the dangers of complacency – not being worried because things seem to be going all right. When doubts and loss of faith threaten our spirituality, we might repeat the words of the Council: 'What further testimony do we need? We have heard it ourselves from his own lips.' The challenge is to trust the words of Jesus, who is himself the Word of God.

4. RESPONSE

On the wall behind my desk there is a reproduction of Gerrit van Honthorst's painting (c. 1617) of Jesus before the High Priest, who is seated at a table draped with a heavy cloth, (anachronistic) books open before him, presumably the scriptures, one candle on the table illuminating the faces of Jesus and the high priest and the word of God upon the table. Behind Jesus are the people who have arrested him, spears and weapons held aloft in the dim light around the door. Jesus has his hands bound, his gaze respectful but uncowed, directed on the face of the High Priest, who wags an admonitory left forefinger that catches the light of the candle. Because of his face bent towards the candlelight and his white, if rather dishevelled robe, the figure of Jesus is the most luminous thing in the picture. It seems that Jesus is the light, the one who testifies to the truth, illuminating the surrounding darkness. When he was arrested in the garden, he said, 'This is your hour, and the power of darkness' (22:53). Honthorst's painting is not a particularly Lucan scene, since it depicts an interrogation by night, but presumably Jesus was, however briefly, brought before the high priest when he was arrested, and it helps to focus our thoughts.

Close your eyes and picture the scene, and address your thoughts and prayers to Jesus, who is the light of the world. 'The power of darkness' (Satan) is trying to get rid of the light, but the light will overcome it. We thank the Lord for the light he brings into the world, and renew our faith that the darkness will never prevail.

You saved Peter, Lord; save us, save all the weak and stumbling disciples who are ill prepared for the time of trial which faces your church at this time. Give us renewed hope through your passion, death and resurrection that your face is shining upon us to save us from our human weakness. Make us prayerful. Help us to take time to be with you in prayer. Help us to trust your word. You are our advocate at the right hand of the Father, where you always pray for us. Do not let us harden our hearts to your gaze of love, or to your brothers and sisters in need. Forgive us for becoming the unjust judges when we judge others harshly, ridicule or hurt people. Nourish us with your word, which fills the empty spaces within us. Help us through illness, or depression. Help us when we must surrender our powers into your hands, let us trust in your goodness. Give us courage to face the journey of life with you to the Father, who is our first beginning and our last end.

5. CONTEMPLATION

Keep this image, in your mind and heart, of Jesus the light faced with the unreceptive world of darkness, but sure that it will be overcome. The light of Jesus' word cannot be extinguished. Let his light shine in us, with confidence in his saving presence. Live with the knowledge that his face is turned to us in love and compassion, that he prays for us always. Lord, let your face shine, that we may be saved. Choose a text to ponder in your heart: 'The Lord turned and looked at Peter'; or 'From now on the Son of Man will be seated at the right hand of the power of God.'

Prayer:

God our Father, your Word, Jesus the Christ, spoke peace and truth to a world of darkness, and brought to humanity the gift of repentance and forgiveness, through the suffering and death he endured. Teach us, the people who bear his name, to follow the example he gave us; may our faith, hope and charity turn hatred to love, conflict to peace, death to eternal life. We ask this through Christ our Lord. Amen
(Adapted from the Roman Missal, Fourth Sunday of Lent, B)

Session 18 The Crucifixion of Jesus (Luke 23:33-49)

1. FOCUS

Take time to focus the mind and heart on the presence of the Lord. For suggestions see Introduction p 18 or Session 1 p 26.

Prayer:

> Lord Jesus, help us to contemplate your cross so that we may learn the lessons of your passion and death. Help us to seek forgiveness through the power of your cross, and to offer forgiveness with generosity, as you did to those who crucified you. Teach us to accept the Father's will with love and obedience, and with your help to entrust ourselves to God our Father, now and at the hour of our death. Amen.

2. FAMILIARISATION

Read the text a few times to become familiar with it. Try to remember this sequence: (1) The crucifixion is very briefly described, Jesus prays for forgiveness for those responsible for his death, and is mocked; (2) dramatic story of forgiveness by Jesus; (3) Jesus gives himself into the Father's hands; (4) positive reactions to his death. Close your eyes and recall the sequence.

Crucified with sinners

> 23:33 When they came to the place that is called The Skull, they crucified Jesus there,
> with the criminals, one on his right and one on his left.
> 34 Then Jesus said, 'Father, forgive them;
> for they do not know what they are doing.'
> And they cast lots to divide his clothing.
> 35 And the people stood by, watching;
> but the leaders scoffed at him, saying,
> 'He saved others; let him save himself,
> if he is the Messiah of God, his chosen one!'
> 36 The soldiers also mocked him,
> coming up and offering him sour wine,
> 37 and saying, 'If you are the King of the Jews, save yourself!'
> 38 There was also an inscription over him,
> 'This is the King of the Jews.'

The Crucified One saves sinners

    39 One of the criminals who were hanged there
    kept deriding him and saying,
    'Are you not the Messiah? Save yourself and us!'
    40 But the other rebuked him, saying, 'Do you not fear God,
    since you are under the same sentence of condemnation?
    41 And we indeed have been condemned justly,
    for we are getting what we deserve for our deeds,
    but this man has done nothing wrong.
    42 Then he said,
    'Jesus, remember me when you come into your kingdom.'
    43 He replied,
    'Truly, I tell you, today you will be with me in Paradise.'

Father, into your hands

    44 It was now about noon, and darkness
    came over the whole land until three in the afternoon,
    45 while the sun's light failed;
    and the curtain of the temple was torn in two.
    46 Then Jesus, crying with a loud voice, said,
    'Father, into your hands I commend my spirit.'
    Having said this, he breathed his last.

Contemplation of the cross

    47 When the centurion saw what had taken place,
    he praised God and said, 'Certainly this man was innocent.'
    48 And when all the crowds who had gathered there
    for this spectacle saw what had taken place,
    they returned home, beating their breasts.
    49 But all his acquaintances,
    including the women who had followed him from Galilee,
    stood at a distance, watching these things.

2.1. Background
Leaders should be familiar with this material before leading a group.
All group members are strongly encouraged to read the text and the
background notes before coming to a group session.
2.1.1 Comparison with Mark: Luke has reordered Mark's sequence,
with omissions and additions. He omits some of the mockery (in
particular, references to Jesus' words about destruction of the

temple, omitted in Luke's trial scene); the words of desolation ('My God, my God, why have you forsaken me?'), and accompanying reference to Elijah. He adds Jesus asking the Father's forgiveness for his executioners, the offer of Paradise to the sinner on the cross, the curtain of the temple torn before Jesus' death (it comes *after* his death in Mark 15:38 and Matthew 25:51), the contemplation of the cross by the crowd, who go away beating their breasts. Luke therefore tries to soften the desolation of the cross, stresses Jesus' prayerful and obedient closeness to the Father, and puts a theology of the meaning of the cross into Jesus' words.

2.1.2 There is a *quasi-liturgical character* to Luke's presentation. Jesus in a priestly gesture offers himself into the hands of his Father, seeks forgiveness for those who sin against him through ignorance, is confident that he can offer Paradise to the repentant sinner. This is Jesus who entered the temple, cleansed it and took possession of it, fulfilling Malachi 3:1, 'The Lord whom you are seeking will suddenly come to his temple'. Jesus is completing the offering made by Mary and Joseph at the Presentation in the temple (2:22-38). On the cross he is surrounded by people contemplating his death, for whom it is a conversion experience – they leave beating their breasts.

2.1.3 *The death of Stephen (Acts 7:55-60)* is modelled on that of Jesus. He offered himself into the hands of Jesus and prayed for forgiveness for his executioners. The message of Luke is clear: every follower of Jesus should imitate Jesus when it comes to that important moment.

2.1.4 *Theology in story form:* What is the meaning of Jesus' death on the cross? The words of Jesus at the Last Supper have already clarified what is happening on the cross, 'This is my body which is given for you … this cup that is poured out for you is the new covenant in my blood' (22:19f). The two who were crucified with Jesus, called 'robbers' in Mark/Matthew, really a mistranslation of *lestoi*, 'terrorists', are called 'wrongdoers', *kakourgoi*, in Luke. Jesus referred to this at the end of the Last Supper story, 22:37, saying that the prophecy from the great Suffering Servant Song, Isaiah 53:12, 'He was counted among the lawless', has to be fulfilled in him. Luke's use of this prophecy makes it clear that he is using the motif of the Servant of God, whose death benefits others, to interpret the crucifixion, even though he does not quote the verse about his life given in ransom for others, as Matthew and Mark do (see Session 15, Last Supper, 2.1.3). He puts his theology in story form: one of the evildoers appeals to Jesus on the cross and is offered Paradise. The meaning of the cross is clear: to anyone who puts faith in Jesus crucified and prays to him with repentance, Jesus on the cross is able to offer eternal life.

2.1.5 Jesus the Saviour: Some commentators doubt that Luke has any theology of Jesus offering himself in sacrifice on the cross. They claim that Jesus gives us an example, that Jesus is a heroic martyr who calls us all to trust God and give ourselves into his hands no matter what. Of course the example of Jesus is rich in meaning and challenges us to imitate him. But to restrict Luke's understanding of the cross to good example is a very shallow understanding of his theology. In fact, of all the gospels, Luke is the one who presents Jesus as making a priestly offering of his life for us, using the theology of the Servant of God from Isaiah. Prayerful reflection on Luke's use of saviour and the verb to save, on the Last Supper, and the crucifixion, leaves little doubt about Luke's profound theology of Jesus' saving death.

2.1.6 The centurion (more historically) in Luke reacts to the death of Jesus by saying, 'Certainly this man was innocent.' Mark seems to put on his lips the later faith of the Christian community, 'Truly this man was God's Son' (Mark 15:39).

3. REFLECTION
Take a period of quiet to digest the text. The leader may invite those who feel comfortable with it to say briefly what initially strikes them about the passage. Use the 4 keys to reflect on the crucifixion according to Luke.

3.1 Journey: Remember 9:31, 'speaking of his departure (exodus) which he was to accomplish at Jerusalem'; and 9:51, 'when the days drew near for him to be taken up (*analempsis*, 'assumption', a noun from the verb Luke uses for the ascension in Acts), he set his face to go to Jerusalem.' Jesus on the cross actively offers himself into the hands of his Father, who will complete the journey by 'lifting him up' in the resurrection.

3.2 Joy: There is great sadness, of course. However, reasons for deep joy: we know from the Last Supper that the blood of Jesus spilled is 'covenant blood', that his giving of himself to the Father is 'for us', and his prayer for forgiveness of those who crucify him extends to us all. We are to draw hope from the scene where the repentant wrongdoer on the cross makes his incredible act of faith in Jesus and finds out about the power of Jesus crucified. Contemplation of the cross leads to repentance, and those who repent receive from Jesus the promise of Paradise.

3.3 Personal:
Jesus: note first the close relationship between Jesus and the Father, even on the cross. 'Father, forgive them ...' (v 34); and 'Father, into your hands I commend my spirit' (a quotation of Psalm 31:5 with the addition of 'Father') v 46. Before the final cry, the curtain of the temple is torn in two (Mark and Matthew have this happen as a result of Jesus' death): the meaning seems to be that the curtain, which hung before the Holy of Holies and could only be entered by the High Priest once a year to make the offering on the Day of Atonement, is opened up to Jesus (and therefore to us) as he offers himself on the cross. Then note Jesus' care for those around him, for those who have brought him to this cross. He pleads with the Father for their forgiveness. To the repentant sinner, he offers no word of rebuke or judgement, only the offer of sharing his place in Paradise. Luke has this lovely way of conveying profound meaning through story and symbol: one man's personal salvation story gives us all hope of salvation.

The bystanders: the cross becomes a source of contemplation and conversion. 'The people (*laos*, the people of God) stood by, 'watching' (v 35). Luke uses the verb *theorein* for 'watching', with the meaning of 'careful studied observation', contemplation. After they have watched it all, they show repentance: when 'the crowds ... saw what had taken place, they returned home, beating their breasts' (v 48). His friends, including the women disciples, stood watching (*theorein*). The centurion, a Roman soldier in charge of the crucifixion, praises God when he sees how Jesus dies, and proclaims his innocence. Luke therefore puts be-

BLESSED BE THE LORD

fore us the need to contemplate the cross, to learn praise of God and the way to salvation. Take a little time to 'watch' the scene on the cross, and pay attention to your feelings as the events unfold.

3.4 *Challenge:* The supreme challenge is the example of Jesus teaching us how to live and die. Stephen in Acts (7:55-60) imitates his Master in death, forgiving his killers and handing himself into the hands of Jesus. Followers of Jesus learn how to approach their own exodus to the Father, trusting in God. We are likewise challenged to contemplate the cross, to learn from it the meaning of the offering of Jesus and the salvation that he offers us, if we come to him with humility and faith. Jesus is challenged (vv 35, 39) to save himself as a sign: he refuses to save himself and becomes through that refusal the Saviour of others. We remember his words, that those who seek to save their own lives lose them (9:24). He calls us to unselfish love and service. Jesus' forgiveness on the cross challenges us to look at our relationships and unresolved tensions, and to learn to forgive, to pray for those who may have hurt us.

4. RESPONSE

It would be useful to identify with the 'watchers' in the text, be one of those who 'beat their breasts'.

Watch Jesus identified with sinners, and his first words about forgiveness. How do you feel about this? Do you feel that he identifies with you? How do you respond prayerfully to that feeling? You may pray firstly for a share in that forgiveness which Jesus wants for you, for healing and acceptance. 'This man welcomes sinners (15:2).' Respond to his welcome. *From your cross, Lord, may your healing mercy wash away our failures and weaknesses, the shameful times when we denied you. Thank you for welcoming us into your presence.* Do you feel that there are people you need to forgive at this time? Are there relationship problems which need healing? *Father, we forgive all who have injured us, small and petty slights compared to what Jesus suffered. Give us hearts ready to forgive.*

Watch people scoffing at Jesus. How do you react? We may allow scoffers to intimidate us into silence, or be too angry with them. How does Jesus react? Do you feel you can pray for them?

Can we say with Jesus, 'Father, forgive them, they do not know what they are doing?'

Watch the 'wrongdoers' on their crosses with Jesus, and their different reactions. One reacts in the all too human way that we often do ourselves, with anger and harsh words, missing the moment. The other makes an enormous leap of faith. Does he give you hope? Thank God for the example of that dying man on the cross, and the total love with which Jesus answered him. If you feel a very 'ordinary' person, are you able to put your trust in the power of Jesus crucified like the 'wrongdoer' on the cross? *Lord Jesus, crucified for me, I put my total trust in you, not in myself. Help me never to fear even death itself, since you make the promise of paradise to everyone who trusts in you. Give me the grace to keep my eyes on you when I approach death, and the grace to ask you to remember me.*

Watch the darkness surround the dying Jesus. The sun fails as the Son is dying. Watch the curtain that hides the Holy of Holies torn in two, opening up the presence of the Father to the crucified humanity of Jesus, and to all who trust in him. Watch Jesus handing himself into the hands of his Father. We know he is doing that for us as well as for himself. Remember his words at the Last Supper: 'This is my body, which is given for you' (22:19). Respond as you feel the need, or just contemplate the scene. Luke is telling us that Jesus is our high priest, robed in the truly priestly garments of love and obedience, giving himself to the Father that we might have hope. *Father, we unite ourselves to Jesus, who shares his priesthood with us in baptism, and we offer ourselves to you in union with his offering. Help us to live in continual remembrance of this great act of saving mercy by uniting ourselves with the Eucharistic offering which he asked us to make in his memory.*

5. CONTEMPLATION

Luke tells us how to do this. Contemplate the cross with the watchers in the gospel, the crowds, his acquaintances, the women disciples. Contemplating the cross, they beat their breasts. Contemplation of the cross leads to repentance, humility and trust. Try then to live with an awareness of Jesus' love for us and God's goodness and mercy. Try to acquire a Eucharistic mentality, uniting ourselves with Jesus who gives himself into the Father's hands for us.

Choose a text to keep in your mind and heart: 'Father, forgive them, they do not know what they do', or 'Father, into your hands I commend my spirit.'

Prayer:

Father, in Jesus we are your people; through him we receive your forgiveness; with him we offer ourselves to you, in praise and thanksgiving for your saving goodness. Teach us to contemplate your Son's death on the cross, so that we may learn humility, forgiveness, and trust in your eternal goodness. We ask this through Jesus Christ, your beloved Son, our Lord, who lives and reigns with you and the Holy Spirit, for ever and ever. Amen.

O King of the Friday
whose limbs were stretched on the cross,
O Lord who did suffer
the bruises, the wounds, the loss,
we stretch ourselves
beneath the shield of thy might.
Some fruit from the tree of thy passion
fall on us this night!
(from the Irish)

Session 19: The Empty Tomb (Luke 23:54–24:12)

1. FOCUS
Take time to focus the mind and heart on the presence of the Lord. For suggestions see Introduction p 18 or Session 1 p 26.

Prayer:

> Heavenly Father, God of mercy, we no longer look for Jesus among the dead, for we believe that you have raised him up and made him the Lord of life. From the waters of death you raise us with him and renew your gift of life within us. Increase in our minds and hearts the risen life we share with Christ, and help us to grow as your people towards the fulness of eternal life with you. We ask this through Christ our Lord. Amen. *(Second Sunday of Easter, adapted)*

2. FAMILIARISATION
Read the text a few times carefully. A portion of the burial story is included as introduction, because the women disciples, who 'watched' all that happened at Jesus' death and burial, provide the link to the story of the finding of the empty tomb. Close your eyes and think of the sequence of events in your mind.

Women disciples watch the burial of Jesus
> 23:54 It was the day of preparation,
> and the Sabbath was beginning.
> 55 The women who had come with him from Galilee followed,
> and they saw the tomb and how his body was laid.
> 56 Then they returned and prepared spices and ointments.
> On the Sabbath day they rested
> according to the commandment.

The women find the tomb empty, and hear the Easter Proclamation
> 24:1 But on the first day of the week, at early dawn,
> they came to the tomb, taking the spices they had prepared.
> 2 They found the stone rolled away from the tomb,
> 3 but when they went in, they did not find the body.
> 4 While they were perplexed about this,
> suddenly two men in dazzling clothes stood beside them.

5 The women were terrified
and bowed their faces to the ground,
but the men said to them,
'Why do you look for the living among the dead?
He is not here, but has risen [has been raised].
6 Remember how he told you, while he was still in Galilee,
7 that the Son of Man must be handed over to sinners,
[Lk 9:22] and be crucified, and on the third day rise again.'

The male disciples do not believe the message
8 Then they remembered his words,
9 and, returning from the tomb,
they told all this to the Eleven and to all the rest.
10 Now it was Mary Magdalene, Joanna,
Mary the mother of James, and the other women with them
who told this to the apostles.
11 But these words seemed to them an idle tale,
and they did not believe them.
12 But Peter got up and ran to the tomb;
stooping and looking in,
he saw the linen cloths by themselves; then he went home,
amazed [wondering] at what had happened.

2.1 Background

Group leaders should study the background notes before leading a session. All group members are strongly encouraged to read the text and the background notes before coming to a meeting. Note that 2.1.1 to 2.1.4 are general comments on the resurrection narratives rather than specific to the text of the finding of the empty tomb.

2.1.1 The empty tomb does not of itself serve as a proof of the resurrection. Even in early Christianity there were allegations that the body had not been buried there (condemned criminals were usually thrown into a common grave), or that the body had been stolen. The stories of the finding of the empty tomb are combined with an 'Easter Proclamation' (see 2.1.6). In Luke this comes from the two young men in dazzling clothes. This heavenly announcement varies in wording, but always has the declaration that Jesus is alive. This announcement usually convinces those who receive it, but they find difficulty convincing anyone else on this basis alone. It was the appearances of the risen Jesus to the disciples that led to faith in the resurrection. Nevertheless the fact that the tomb was empty is vital: without it there would have been no preaching of the resurrection, for if the body had been still in the tomb, no one would have believed the message. So the empty tomb is an essential underpinning of faith in the resurrection. The thinking of the people of the Holy Land at that time (groups of Jews in Egypt and elsewhere may have been more influenced by Greek ideas) was only very slightly influenced by the Greek understanding that each person consists of a material body that perishes and a spiritual soul that lives on. Though this idea pervades all western Europe, in Judaea and Galilee resurrection meant the resurrection of the person, including the body, though in a new dimension of being. Jesus experienced death and resurrection in his human body, and the risen Jesus retains his humanity eternally. So we are not speaking only of Jesus' soul living on, or of Jesus living on in his divine nature. Some modern liberal Christians say it would not matter to their faith if the bones of Jesus were found in Jerusalem, but it would have seriously mattered to the first Christians and those who wished to prove them wrong.

2.1.2 Rediscovery of the full meaning of the resurrection for our salvation was one of the great breakthroughs of the 1950s and 1960s, though it has taken a long time to trickle down to many of us reared in the old way of thinking. In the first half of the 20th century, the emphasis was on the redemptive suffering and death of Jesus. The resurrection was seen chiefly as a *proof* that Jesus was who he said he was, and as a sign that one day we would share in the eternal life of the resurrection. In the second half of the century, studies of scripture and early church teaching showed that we were saved by the passion, death *and resurrection* of Jesus. They are all part of the one movement, the Paschal Mystery, in Luke's language the exodus of Jesus to the Father. Romans 4:24-25 says: '… believe in him who raised Jesus our Lord from the dead, who was handed over to death for our trespasses and was raised for our justification.' The risen Lord is life-giver, sharing his new life with his people, winning for us the gift of the Holy Spirit, and remaining in his glorified humanity our high priest, interceding for us in the presence of the Father.

2.1.3 No one observed the resurrection. It is a divine event, and all
we can say about its timing is that it happened between the closing of the tomb on the Friday and the finding of the empty tomb
on Easter Sunday. Resurrection is not coming back to life as before (like Lazarus). Jesus passes to a new kind of life, outside the
bounds of history, time and physics. He is now alive in the presence of the Father. We can only imagine the reception of Jesus'
risen humanity into the infinite love of the Father, the transform-
ation of his broken body, the clothing of his risen humanity in the
fulness of the life of the Spirit. We can only imagine his human joy
in the power he now has to intercede with the Father for all his
people, to bring forgiveness and healing to his disciples. Though
living now beyond our human dimensions, he is able to 'appear'
visibly to any person or group of people, anywhere. His presence
is life-giving, healing, forgiving, empowering for those who believe in him, who 'see the Lord', i.e., experience his power.

2.1.4 Spiritual implications: All this has rich implications for our
spiritual lives and for our prayer. Since we share now in the life
of the risen Christ and the life of the Spirit, which unites us to the
Father and to each other, we have a rich inner life to enjoy, to celebrate and to deepen through our prayer and our Christian living. We do not forget the passion and death of Jesus. The risen
Jesus retains the marks of his passion on his body, which seems
puzzling at first. Surely glorification takes away the marks of our
earthly suffering? But it is part of God's plan, so that (a) the disciples should be able to identify the risen Christ, something they
found difficult according to the appearance narratives, and (b) so
that we may always see the risen Christ as the one whose self-
giving for us is continuous, who is still offering himself for us in
love in the presence of the Father and in the Eucharist. The risen
Lord in all his glory and power comes to us in the Eucharist,
bringing us healing, forgiveness and the gift of the Spirit. The
Lord who came to bring us the fullness of life wishes us to be joyfully alive, to celebrate that life and use the gifts he has so lavish-
ly given us. It is this perspective that made the canticles of the
early chapters of Luke's gospel the church's joyful thanksgiving
for the blessings of salvation. We have tried to allow those canticles to colour our prayerful approach to the gospel.

2.1.5 The women who had come with Jesus from Galilee 'stood at a distance watching' the death of Jesus (23:49), 'and they saw the tomb and how his body was laid' (v 55), i.e. not anointed with the customary burial rites. So they prepare 'spices and ointments', rest on the Sabbath day, and come very early on the first day of the week to the tomb. These faithful women form the link between the death, burial and the empty tomb. They knew where the body was laid, they came with a purpose, to anoint the body. They did not expect to find the tomb empty. In the midst of their grief, they were shocked to find the body missing.

2.1.6 The Easter Proclamation: Matthew, Mark and Luke have a proclamation of the good news of the resurrection in the empty tomb narrative (Matthew, 'an angel of the Lord', 28:5-7; Mark, 'a young man', 16:5-7; Luke, 'two men in dazzling clothes', 24:5-7). The wording differs, but always contains the message: 'He has been raised, he is not here.' In Mark and Matthew there is a commission to go and tell the news to the disciples, with the promise that Jesus will meet them in Galilee. Luke probably knew about the appearances in Galilee, but in his gospel all is centred in Jerusalem. All of the events of Luke chapter 24 take place on the same day, the first day of the week, in Jerusalem. In Luke's geographical thinking, Jesus journeys to Jerusalem for his exodus to the Father, and from Jerusalem the good news of salvation will radiate outwards to the ends of the earth. So the message that they will see Jesus in Galilee becomes a call to remember what Jesus prophesied in Galilee. The young men quote Jesus' prophecy of his suffering, death and rising again from Luke 9:22, with some variations: 'Remember how he told you, while he was still in Galilee, that the Son of Man must be handed over to sinners (9:22 to the elders etc.), and be crucified (9:22 killed), and on the third day rise again. Then they remembered his words' (24:6-8). In chapter 24, Jesus or the words of Jesus are the interpreters of the meaning of the suffering, death and resurrection. The disciples are to listen and learn from him. The women remember and believe, and pass on the message; the men are slow to believe, and think the words of the women are 'an idle tale' (literally, *léros*, from which we get delirious).

2.1.7 Disbelief from the male disciples: They refuse to give any credence to the women's report. Luke shows that the original preachers of the resurrection were not rushed into faith, and had preconceptions against it. If they had understood Jesus' words about rising from the dead at all, they would have understood them in terms of the general resurrection of the dead at the judgement day, not an immediate resurrection.

3. REFLECTION
Now we are ready to reflect prayerfully on the text. Take a period of silence to digest the text. Group leaders may invite those who feel comfortable with it to share briefly initial reactions to the text.

3.1 Journey: Jesus' journey to the Father is now accomplished, and his joy will be to pour out the resulting blessings on his disciples. His first gift will be faith, which will begin from the finding of the empty tomb, the remembering of what he said, and then meeting the risen Lord, followed by the gift of the Spirit. The journey to understanding will not be smooth for the disciples. It begins with the faithful women going to the tomb at first light on Easter Sunday morning, to anoint the body of Jesus. They hear the Easter Proclamation, which for Luke recapitulates the journey of Jesus to the Father, Jesus' prophecy of his 'exodus' (9:31) and his 'lifting up' (9:51). The women, remembering and beginning to understand, make quick progress on the journey to faith. The male disciples are unbelieving, even Peter, who verifies that the body is missing, and 'wonders with himself', as yet without understanding. Where am I on this journey, not just to faith but to experiencing within me the power of the risen Christ? A stage on the journey may be remembering – how I had stronger, perhaps more joyful faith when I was younger, and in that remembering, rekindling my faith in the wonder of it. 'Wonder and awe in God's presence' is one of the gifts of the Spirit that I used to appreciate more. What needs refreshing, Easter blooming, a new springtime in my faith? The tomb is empty, bringing a surge of hope even to those in grief.

3.2 Joy: The Lord wants us to have joy, and where can we find it more readily than in reliving with the disciples the discovery that Jesus is alive and life-giving? We have to rediscover that

Jesus is alive in us. What if we look into our inner self and find it empty – 'He is not here'? God forbid that I might be looking for the Living One in the deadness of my own heart. When the women came to the tomb, two things stood in their way to finding that Jesus was alive: the stone, and their expectations. God rolled away the stone, and the proclamation of the two young men helped them to overcome their low expectations. The NRSV text has 'He is not here, but has risen.' A better translation is 'He has been raised', that is, by the Father, which fits better with the early description of the resurrection as the work of God the Father, raising up Jesus. God our Father wants to remove all obstacles to our joy in the risen Christ, obstacles outside us and obstacles inside us. Are there obstacles which keep us from experiencing the joy of the resurrection? If, like the male disciples, we are as yet finding it hard to find Easter joy, let us beg the Father to help us to meet the risen Jesus and experience his joy within us. This is the day the Lord has made, let us rejoice and be glad.

3.3 Personal: The deep personal commitment of the women to Jesus leads them back to the tomb, where they will receive a personal revelation. Note their moods of perplexity, terror, hearing a message of hope, remembering, running to tell, frustration because they are not believed. When our moods are dark, the personal commitment to Jesus is what each of us needs. Keep faithful, be patient with unbelief, your own and that of others. Peter's commitment makes him go to see, and leads to wondering. We never know what the Lord will do for us if we search and begin to wonder!

3.4 Challenge: Our challenge is to have faith in the Risen Jesus and to bring the message to others, as the women disciples do; to remember the Lord's words and savour them; to rejoice that the Lord is alive; to grow in courage from that realisation.

Many can easily share in the frustration of the women trying to bring the good news to others who have not 'seen' or heard. We must be patient. We begin to understand how difficult is the act of faith in this uncertain and distracting world. We must do our best and leave the rest in the Lord's hands. We have been disciples following Jesus on his journey to Jerusalem; now we do need to be part of the journey of the word to the ends of the earth. St Patrick saw Ireland as 'the ends of the earth', and there is work to be done there again. Finally we must be disciples following him on his journey to the Father, ready to give ourselves into the Father's hands. We know that will mean sharing in his dying as well as sharing in his resurrection. We must grow in courage through the knowledge that Jesus is alive and with us.

4. RESPONSE

We must each of us make our personal response to the good news of the resurrection of Jesus. Exult, if you can, be joyful, give thanks and praise for the hope that the resurrection gives us. Ask for renewed faith if necessary. Resolve to strive for a commitment to Jesus like the faithful women who found the tomb empty and began to spread the news. Ask for courage to follow Jesus in his 'exodus' to the Father. When we come to death, may we be able to offer ourselves with him to the Father; may the Father raise us up to new life with him. Rejoice in our present sharing in the new life of the resurrection.

5. CONTEMPLATION

We are Easter people. We wish to live in an awareness of the presence of the Risen Lord in us and around us. Keep saying the words, 'He is not here, he has been raised.' 'Why do you look for the living among the dead?' Take a stroll in your local cemetery, not to be sad or morbid, but to glory in the power of God who raises the dead to everlasting glory.

Prayer:

Lord Jesus Christ, by your own three days in the tomb, you made holy the graves of all who believe in you, and so made the grave a sign of hope that promises resurrection even as it claims our mortal bodies. Grant to our deceased loved ones the joy of the resurrection, for you are the resurrection and the life. May they see you face to face and in your light see light, and know the splendour of God, for you are alive and reign for ever and ever. Amen.

(*Adapted from* The Order of Christian Funerals, *Veritas 1991*)

Session 20: Journey to Emmaus (Luke 24 :13-35)

1. FOCUS
Take time to focus mind and heart on the presence of God. For suggestions see Introduction p 18 or Session 1 p 26.

Prayer:

> Lord Jesus, when your disciples were filled with the disappointment of hopes dashed on Calvary, you walked with them and gave them back hope and joy. Lord, walk with us when we are in distress and darkness, nourish us with your word and with your eucharistic presence, that we may follow you with eagerness and determination, knowing that you are always with us, who live and reign for ever and ever. Amen.

2. FAMILIARISATION
This is a very familiar story, so read it carefully with fresh eyes, paying attention to the different stages of the narrative as headlined. Retell the story to yourself – a good way of finding out what you have missed! Then read it again.

Journey of discovery

> 24:13 Now on that same day two of them
> were going to a village called Emmaus,
> about seven miles from Jerusalem,
> 14 and talking with each other
> about all these things that had happened.
> 15 While they were talking and discussing,
> Jesus himself came near and went with them,
> 16 but their eyes were kept from recognising him.
> 17 And he said to them, 'What are you discussing
> with each other while you walk along?'
> They stood still, looking sad.

Telling their story

> 18 Then one of them, whose name was Cleopas,
> answered him. 'Are you the only stranger in Jerusalem
> who does not know the things that have taken place
> in these days?'

19 He asked them, 'What things?'
They replied, 'The things about Jesus of Nazareth,
who was a prophet mighty in deed and word
before God and all the people,
20 and how our chief priests and leaders handed him over
to be condemned to death and crucified him.
21 But we had hoped that he was the one to redeem Israel.
Yes, and besides all this,
it is now the third day since these things took place.
22 Moreover, some women of our group astounded us.
They were at the tomb early this morning,
23 and when they did not find his body there,
they came back and told us that they had indeed seen
a vision of angels who said that he was alive.
24 Some of those who were with us went to the tomb
and found it exactly as the women had said;
but they did not see him.'

The story retold, rethought.
25 Then he said to them,
'Oh, how foolish you are,
and how slow of heart to believe
all that the prophets have declared!
26 Was it not necessary that the Messiah
should suffer these things and then enter into his glory?'
27 Then beginning with Moses and all the prophets,
he interpreted to them the things about himself
in all the scriptures.

Recognition
28 As they came near the village to which they were going,
he walked ahead of them as if he were going on.
29 But they urged him strongly, saying,
'Stay with us, because it is almost evening
and the day is now nearly over.'
So he went in to stay with them.
30 When he was at the table with them, he took bread,
blessed [said the blessing], and broke it, and gave it to them.
31 Then their eyes were opened,
and they recognised him; and he vanished from their sight.

32 They said to each other,
'Were not our hearts burning within us
while he was talking to us on the road,
while he was opening the scriptures to us?'

Sharing the new story

33 That same hour they got up and returned to Jerusalem;
and they found the eleven and their companions
gathered together.
34 They were saying,
'The Lord has risen indeed, and he has appeared to Simon!'
35 Then they told what had happened on the road,
and how he had been made known to them
in the breaking of bread.

2.1 Background

Group leaders should make themselves familiar with this before meeting the group. Other members of a group are strongly encouraged to read the text and the background notes before coming to a group session.

2.1.1 It is Easter Sunday: 'on that same day' (v 13) refers to the women going to the tomb early on the first day of the week, and finding it empty. All of the events of chapter 24 take place within one day, our Easter Sunday.

2.1.2 Where was Emmaus? There is uncertainty about the correct text for 'seven miles from Jerusalem' (*lit.* 60 stadia, 7 miles; a variant reading gives 160 stadia, over 18 miles). There are three possible locations for the town, so the village visited by tourist bus trips is merely the place where the event is remembered. Seven miles seems a more realistic walking distance from Jerusalem, given that they returned the same evening.

2.1.3 Lack of recognition: The risen Jesus walks with disciples without being recognised. There is a moment of unrecognition in nearly all the resurrection stories. Jesus has not just come back to life as he was before; he is not going to be with them in the old way. He is already in glory, and it is 'from glory' that he appears to his disciples (see Background for session 21, 2.1.5). It requires faith to 'see' him, to grasp what is happening. It is only when the disciples listened to their own story retold from a different perspective, and saw his familiar gestures in the breaking of bread, that their eyes were opened, and they recognised him, or, as v 35 has it, 'he had been made known to them', i.e. by God. Then he is no longer visible to physical eyes, but they have 'seen' and understand that he is with them in his word and in the 'breaking of bread'.

2.1.4 Presence of Jesus: How do we recognise the presence of the Risen Jesus? Luke wants to instruct Theophilus (and us). So he has given a quasi-liturgical setting to the narrative. Jesus is with us even when we do not know it; he is with us in his word, and in the breaking of bread, the Eucharist. So we have a 'liturgy of the word', where Jesus interprets the scriptures, and a 'breaking of bread'. We may have an open mind as to whether Luke intended it to be a Eucharist, but he certainly intended to recall the gestures of Jesus at the Last Supper, and to remind us of the presence of the Risen Jesus in the Eucharist. It requires faith to 'see' him, and our hearts need to be set on fire by prayerful reflection on the scriptures and on the story of Jesus for us to be able to 'see' properly and recognise him.

2.1.5 Jesus interprets the scriptures: Here and in the next appearance to the apostles (24:36-49), and again in the beginning of Acts, Luke stresses that the Christian understanding of the death and resurrection of Jesus came from the Lord himself. Jesus taught them how to interpret the scriptures. 'Moses and all the prophets' (v 27) includes the Pentateuch (the 5 books of Moses), the historical books (called the 'Former Prophets'), and the 'Latter Prophets', the prophets as we know them. V 44 is more inclusive: 'Everything written about me in the law of Moses, the prophets, and the psalms must be fulfilled.' In particular, this means that the Christian understanding of Messiah includes areas of the scriptures which Jews never associate(d) with the Messiah, especially the Songs of the Suffering Servant in Second Isaiah, and the psalms (laments) of the just one wrongly persecuted, whom God will vindicate (e.g. Ps 22 'My God, my God, why have you forsaken me?' quoted by Jesus on the cross in Mark and Matthew, though not in Luke).

2.1.6 The necessity of suffering: (compare Session 16, Background,

2.1.4). 'Was it not necessary that the Messiah should suffer these things and then enter into his glory?' (v 26). We need to be careful not to interpret this 'necessity' as a demand of a stern God that his Son must suffer. The necessity is that Jesus must carry out his mission even if it leads to his death. The experience of the prophets showed that those who speak God's truth are going to meet opposition and possible death. There is no possibility of Jesus changing his message to avoid human violence or diabolic attack. Jesus lovingly accepts all the opposition his mission provokes. There is also a certain fittingness that he takes upon himself all the evils to which humanity is subject, and so has entered into human suffering in order to redeem it, and show us how suffering can become life-giving, the seed that perishes to provide new growth (John 12:24).

3. REFLECTION (AND RESPONSE)
This is a beautiful and well-known text, and leaders may wish to invite members of a group, after a period of silent reflection, to share briefly with others their reactions to the text, before considering the 'keys'.
Note: Because of the importance of our responding to the Risen Jesus, I have chosen to build the necessary Response of prayer into each stage of the reflection. So take time to pray quietly after considering any or each of the key words.

3.1 *Journey:* It is a true pilgrim journey, though initially a journey away from a holy place, but still to a place where they find Jesus and inspiration, and return to Jerusalem with new insight. The two disciples set out with questions but little hope of answers. It is a journey away from hope: 'We had hoped that he was the one to redeem Israel' (v 21). They express their disappointment and can make no sense even of the women saying they found the tomb empty. They are asked to tell their story to a stranger, and this stranger retells the story so that it makes new sense – it is only later that they realise how heart-warming this new understanding is. They press the stranger to stay with them, and they recognise that he is Jesus in the breaking of the bread. Then they return immediately to Jerusalem to share the story. They will have travelled about 14 miles, but a much longer distance on the inward journey of faith.

Response

The material for our prayer is thanksgiving to God for the realisation that Jesus always walks with us, in the midst of doubts and personal trials, even when we do not recognise him. Pray firstly that we may never doubt the reality of Jesus' living presence in our lives, that we may never ignore or be indifferent to that living presence. He invites us to tell our story, and to listen for his word that helps us to make sense of it. In prayer, confide your personal fears and anxieties to the listening Lord, who treats disciples, even those going in the wrong direction, very gently. Ask him to help you to understand what is happening in your life at this time. Pray also for others about whom you may be concerned, who may be having doubts about their faith. What are your feelings about 'pilgrimage'? Is visiting holy places only about looking for 'cures' for sickness of body, or with Jesus' help can we find other types of healing? What type of healing do you feel most in need of at this time? Pray for it. Would you be happy with 'hearts burning within us', renewed purpose and enthusiasm for your faith?

3.2 *Joy:* I suppose the greatest joy comes after the greatest disappointment. After their despondency, the two disciples listened to the stranger telling them how to interpret the scripture texts that gave the life and death of Jesus new meaning, and recovered hope. When they realised in the breaking of bread that they were actually talking to the living Jesus, their joy was unbounded. It was a heart-warming experience for the two disciples, and it is a heart-warming story for us also. We can empathise with the gloom of the two disciples, and we too have periods of gloom and need moments of spiritual insight and reassurance to get us going again. Joy nourishes our faith and sustains us. But we need to learn from their experience: they spoke out about what was really happening to them, they gave honest voice to their disappointment. Then they listened to the word of the Lord, as interpreted by Jesus. They begged him to stay with them, and asked him to share their meal. It was only then that 'their eyes were opened, and they recognised him.' So joy does not always come easily; we have to work for it, pray with honesty, listen with patience, beg the Lord to stay with us, and share in the 'breaking of bread'.

Response

The beginning of worship is the feeling of being blessed, and the need to give thanks for those blessings. I always feel blessed by this story. Do you? I feel the need to say sorry to the Lord for so often feeling down, and putting a bad face on my Christian faith. I feel the need to thank the Lord for not giving up on me, for being there at my side, for listening to me, for patiently cajoling me out of the glooms, for rekindling my joy. The resurrection of the Lord still makes me want to stand up and applaud. I thank the Risen Lord for his presence within us, for his presence in my brothers and sisters, for the word of God which warms my heart, for his presence in the Eucharist. Would you like to think of one or two things that have brought you joy in recent times, even though those times may have been fraught with difficulties, and to give thanks for those blessings?

3.3 Personal: Luke is a master of this type of narrative, describing how Jesus reaches out to people, starts from where they are, and draws them slowly into a close and heart-warming relationship with himself. These are not two of the 'big name' disciples; he walks with the little ones also. Jesus allows people to walk away from him, but he never abandons them. He walks with them, allowing his presence to be gradually recognised. He is always calling us to closer relationship with himself. We are able to have a very close personal relationship with the living Jesus, present in our hearts, present in his word, present in the Eucharist. Sometimes we have to go through a period of sadness or loss of faith, or loss of enthusiasm for our faith or our work for God, in order to hear the call to a new stage, a new way of praying, or a rediscovery of what we already knew but had forgotten. Jesus' patient love allows the two disciples to grow from despair to hope to joy. His love does the same for us.

Response

Lord, help us to spend more time in your presence, with your word, and with the Eucharist. Help us to grow closer to you, to trust your love and your call to understand better the mysteries of your death and resurrection. How do you feel about your present relationship to Jesus? Rejoice in it, ask the Lord to walk with you. Ask him to give you time to come to terms with disappointments, weariness or illness, the darkness that still lingers within. Lord, lead us through these things by your loving presence, nourish our emptiness, strengthen our faith, fill us with your Easter joy.

3.4 Challenge: This story challenges us to believe that Jesus is risen, walks with us, lives within us. He is listening even when we feel no joy, only tepidity or the absence of God. We are challenged to believe that his will for us, properly understood, is always for our good, that he has shown how suffering can be fruitful, redemptive. The challenge is to rise above our personal troubles and personal grief, or to allow ourselves to be raised by Jesus into hope and joy and purpose. The challenge is to listen to God's word, to allow it to change our mind-set and to recognise Jesus in the breaking of bread. There is challenge to listen to others, to hear their story, to walk with them, as Jesus would like us to do. Think about where you are on your journey now, and whether you are hopeful or dispirited. When was the last time you felt your heart burn within you, and decided to reach out and try to communicate what you felt to others? Do you feel the Lord is challenging you to pass on the message he has graciously brought you to understand and relish? How could you do that? Would you allow your personal joy in the wonder of Jesus' death and resurrection to become a very private thing, smothered by fear and convention?

Response
Thank you, Lord, that we can still get such a spiritual uplift, such psychic energy, from the Emmaus story and others like it. Thank you for your promise to be with us always, and thank you for your presence in your word and in the Eucharist. Stay with us, Lord, for without you we can do nothing. Lord, we beg you for the grace to bounce back from disappointments and life's difficulties. Lord, help us not to give up. Give courage to those who feel disappointed or alone. Grant us the grace to affirm and encourage them. Help us to share the good news with them, not to keep it to ourselves. Help us to bear witness to your resurrection by the way we live, and help us to reach out to others in our community. Give us the grace to be able to build up our community by giving some of our spare time to minister to others in whatever way we can. Help us to share our blessings, with which you so richly grace us.

4. CONTEMPLATION

We are Easter people. The Risen Lord is with us and in us. He shares his risen life with us. We try to live in awareness of this great blessing, remembering that the Risen Lord is with us wherever we go. Choose a text that will remind you of this great truth, and keep it in your heart, e.g. 'Stay with us, because it is almost evening…'; 'Their eyes were opened and they recognised him'.

Prayer:

'Let him easter in us,
be a dayspring to the dimness of us,
be a crimson-cresseted east.'
(G. M. Hopkins)

Come, Holy Spirit, fill the hearts of your faithful, and enkindle in them the fire of your love. Send forth your Spirit, and they shall be created, and you shall renew the face of the earth.

Session 21: The Risen Lord
Commissions his Witnesses (Luke 24:36-53)

1. FOCUS

Take time to focus mind and heart on the presence of the Lord.
For suggestions see Introduction p 18 or Session 1 p 26.

Prayer:

> God our Father, renew our faith and hope through the Risen
> Christ, who opens our minds to your word and calls us to be
> his witnesses. Endow us with the power of the Holy Spirit,
> that we may praise you daily and spread the news that the
> Risen Lord is alive among us. We ask this through the same
> Christ our Lord. Amen.

2. FAMILIARISATION

*Read the text carefully as often as you need to memorise the sequence
of events. Note how Jesus overcomes the doubts of the disciples, how he
teaches them how to give meaning to the terrible events they have lived
through, how he calls them to be witnesses and promises the Spirit before being taken up to heaven – the completion of his 'exodus'.*

Recognising the Lord

> 24:36 While they were talking about this,
> Jesus himself stood among them and said to them,
> 'Peace be with you.'
> 37 They were startled and terrified,
> and thought that they were seeing a ghost.
> 38 He said to them, 'Why are you frightened,
> and why do doubts arise in your hearts?
> 39 Look at my hands and my feet; see that it is I myself.
> Touch me and see;
> for a ghost does not have flesh and bones as you see I have.'
> 40 And when he had said this,
> he showed them his hands and his feet.
> 41 While in their joy they were disbelieving and still wondering,
> he said to them, 'Have you anything here to eat?'
> 42 They gave him a piece of broiled fish,
> 43 and he took it and ate it in their presence.

Interpreting the Scriptures
  44 Then he said to them, 'These are my words
  that I spoke to you while I was still with you –
  that everything written about me in the law of Moses,
  the prophets and the psalms must be fulfilled.'
  45 Then he opened their minds to understand the scriptures.

Commissioning witnesses, and the promise of the Spirit
  46 And he said to them, 'Thus it is written, that the Messiah
  is to suffer and to rise from the dead on the third day,
  47 and that repentance and forgiveness of sins
  is to be proclaimed in his name to all nations,
  beginning from Jerusalem.
  48 You are witnesses of these things.
  49 And see, I am sending upon you
  what my Father promised; so stay here in the city
  until you have been clothed with power from on high.'

Ascension
  50 Then he led them out as far as Bethany,
  and, lifting up his hands, he blessed them.
  51 While he was blessing them,
  he withdrew from them and was carried up into heaven.
  52 And they worshipped him,
  and returned to Jerusalem with great joy;
  53 and they were continually in the temple blessing God.

2.1 Background
Getting to know the background is really part of the familiarisation
process, so that we can pay attention to the intentions of the author in
the passage. Leaders should be familiar with it before leading a session,
but all participants are strongly encouraged to read the text and the
background material before coming to a group session.

2.1.1 Luke's editing of this climactic scene gives it an overall
unity, though it is composed of a number of distinct scenes. It is
the climax of Jesus' journey. He has now completed his exodus
through death and resurrection to the glory of the Father. It is
'from glory' that he appears to his disciples, helps them to recognise that it is really the same Jesus they have known, but in a
new state of being, instructs them on the interpretation of the

scriptures, commissions them, promises that they will be 'clothed with power from on high', then ascends to the Father, leaving them in prayerful praise of God. It will be their task, when they are empowered by the Spirit, to take the message of salvation on the new journey, 'beginning from Jerusalem', to all the nations of the world.

2.1.2 Recognition: It is always a bit surprising that each appearance of the risen Jesus initially meets lack of recognition, even though at least some of the people present are said to have seen him already (Simon, the two disciples at Emmaus), and they have all been excitedly discussing the news (v 36). Do not be surprised, for at least two reasons. Firstly, these narratives have a history as individual resurrection stories, into which the motifs of surprise, lack of recognition, dawning awareness, joy, instruction etc., were woven, before they became part of a continuous narrative. Secondly, Luke is writing not just to record what originally happened, but to foster faith in his readers – remember Theophilus. So there is a theological, even apologetic motif at work, especially for those in the Greek world, for whom bodily resurrection was a difficult idea. He wishes to dispel the notion that Jesus came back to life as before. Resurrection takes Jesus into another state of being outside normal human experience, so it is to be expected that he would not be immediately recognisable. The narrative begins with the appearance of Jesus in the midst of them, greeting them with peace (compare 2:14, the angel's message of peace on earth). But the disciples are frightened, 'startled and terrified, supposing that they saw a spirit'. To reassure them, 'he showed them his hands and his feet', presumably to show the marks of the wounds, though Luke never mentioned the nails in the crucifixion scene (compare John 20:20, 'He showed then his hands and his side' – only John tells us that his side was pierced with a lance). He invited them to touch him, to see that he is 'flesh and bones' and not a disembodied spirit. They still 'disbelieved for joy and wondered' – it is too good to be true! Then he asks for food and eats a piece of cooked fish in their presence. The disciples are literally speechless, there is not a word from them during the whole narrative, and no explicit sign of recognition until v 52, 'They worshipped him, and returned to Jerusalem with great joy'.

2.1.3 Jesus instructs them how to interpret the scriptures. (See Session 20, 2.1.5) Luke repeats here what Jesus said to the disciples on the way to Emmaus, with the addition of a reference to the psalms. No specific references to texts are made, but the Christian interpretation of the scriptural testimony to Jesus will be made more explicit in Acts, especially in the sermons of Peter and Paul. Here Luke stresses again that the Christian interpretation is based on the instruction of the Risen Jesus himself.

2.1.4 Commissioning witnesses: Jesus' interpretation of the scriptures contains the specific message that the Lucan witnesses are to bring from Jerusalem to the nations of the world. In Matthew 28:19 the commission has a Matthean stamp: 'Go and make disciples ... teaching them to observe what I have commanded you.' In Mark 16:15 the command is 'to preach the gospel to every creature'. Luke's Jesus has a message in line with this gospel: 'Thus it is written ... that repentance and forgiveness of sin should be preached in his name to all nations, beginning from Jerusalem' (v 47). The challenge to repent, and the healing mercy of God are to be the foundation of the Christian message. The message characteristically is to go out from Jerusalem in the name of Jesus to all nations. Jesus' followers are to be primarily 'witnesses', and they are not to set off by their own powers, but to wait in Jerusalem to be 'clothed with power from on high'. Jesus says, 'I am sending upon you what my Father promised.' The Holy Spirit is not explicitly mentioned, but is clearly intended; compare Acts 1:4-5, 'He ordered them not to leave Jerusalem, but to wait there for the promise of the Father ... you will be baptised with the Holy Spirit not many days from now.'

2.1.5 Ascension: Luke gives the only really explicit narrative of the ascension. Mark's longer ending has one verse, 16:19, 'The Lord Jesus ... was taken up into heaven and sat down at the right hand of God.' Matthew has no ascension story, John has Jesus tell Mary Magdalene, 'I have not yet ascended to the Father' (20:17), but no account of an ascension. Luke has the only accounts of Jesus' visible ascension, one in the gospel (Easter Sunday), and one in Acts (1:9-11) after his 'appearing to them during forty days and speaking about the kingdom of God'. The early tradition in the New Testament Letters is that Jesus was exalted, raised up by the Father to his own presence, exaltation being the natural consequence of resurrection. 'God put this power to work in Christ when he raised him from the dead and seated him at his right hand in the heavenly places' (Eph 1:20). 'He humbled himself and became obedient to the point of death, even death on a cross. Therefore God also highly exalted him and gave him the name that is above every name ...'(Phil 2:8-9). Without spending too long on the questions which arise, the best approach is to assume that Luke is also aware of the tradition of exaltation, and to accept that each of the appearances in Luke chapter 24 is made 'from glory', visible appearances of the already exalted Christ.

What then is the ascension? It represents an appearance to the disciples which they realised was to be the last of its kind, Jesus' farewell to the disciples, letting them know that he would not be present to them in this visible way again. Having commissioned them to bring his message of repentance and forgiveness of sins to the nations, and having promised them the Holy Spirit, henceforward he would be present in his word, in the Eucharist, and in the power of the Holy Spirit, 'the promise of the Father'.

2.1.6 Blessing and worship: 'He led them out as far as Bethany, and lifting up his hands, he blessed them. While he was blessing them, he withdrew from them and was carried up into heaven.' (vv 50f) Resuming the theme which we noted in the Last Supper and the crucifixion scenes, Jesus now blesses them in a very priestly act. Compare Leviticus 9:22, 'Aaron [the High Priest] lifted his hands towards the people and blessed them; and he came down after sacrificing the sin offering.' Fitzmeyer (Vol 2, p 1590) thinks that 'though Luke depicts Christ performing a hieratic [priestly] act, his theology is not concerned with Jesus as priest.' Perhaps not with priesthood in the Jewish sense, but I feel that by including a priestly action of blessing at this solemn moment, Luke shows that he is indeed concerned with it in a Christian sense, making explicit a theme which can be found in the Last Supper and Crucifixion narratives. Luke never uses the word 'priest' of Jesus, but his way of 'doing theology' is often to build it into the narrative. The disciples now make their explicit gesture of recognition and worship Jesus. Then 'they returned to Jerusalem with great joy, and were continually in the temple blessing God.' So the Gospel reaches a glorious triumph, ends where it began, in the temple, the half doubting of the priestly Zechariah replaced with the joyful praise of God for his blessings, because 'from now on the Son of Man will be seated at the right hand of the power of God' (22:69).

3. REFLECTION
Read the passage again, and allow a period of quiet while you focus on the presence of the Risen Christ and the gift of the Spirit, before you begin to reflect on the passage. Leaders decide when a group is ready to move on, perhaps by allowing some members to speak briefly about the impact of the passage on them.

3.1 Journey: For Jesus the climax of the journey has already come, the completion of his exodus (9:31) to the Father. His prophecy, 'From now on the Son of Man will be seated at the right hand of the power of God' (22:69) is now fulfilled. It is from that glory in the Father's presence that he appears visibly to the disciples. He has to help them first of all to recognise that he is the same Jesus, that they may become comfortable with the strangeness of his risen being. Then he takes them on a learning journey back through what he has said to them already, clarifying the meaning of what they have lived through, helping them to make sense of the journey they have travelled with him. Now there is to be a new journey for them, to be witnesses to him 'to all nations, beginning from Jerusalem'. How will they face this new and frightening journey without his visible presence? They are to stay in Jerusalem until they have been empowered: Jesus will send upon them 'what my Father promised' (Acts 1:4-5 shows that 'the promise of the Father' means 'you will be baptised with the Holy Spirit not many days from now'). Then Jesus led them to Bethany (just over the Mount of Olives), blessed them and 'withdrew from them and was carried up into heaven'. Jesus' ascension has been prepared for by Luke since his use of exodus in the Transfiguration story (9:31), and 'the days … for him to be taken up' (*lit.* of his 'assumption', *analempsis*, 9:51). The ascension is an implicit statement that they will not see him again like this. But such is their new realisation of the wonder of what has happened that they return to Jerusalem, blessing and praising God. Spend a little time thinking about their new mind-set, the change that the appearance of the Risen Jesus has made upon them.

Reflect for a moment on what we have learned on our journey through the gospel with Jesus. We may have been often bewildered like the first disciples, perhaps our complacency has been disturbed, we may be worried at the implications of what we have discovered for our lives as disciples. Now we can sense that we are involved in this commissioning of disciples to be witnesses, that we are invited to be witnesses to Jesus, part of that journey of bringing the news to all nations. What helped the original disciples to change from timidity to courage? It was their graced realisation of the wonder of the drama of salvation, and the promise of the Spirit. We have received the Spirit, but have perhaps lost the wonder after 2000 years. Let us beg the Holy Spirit to renew in us the gift of 'wonder and awe in God's presence'.

3.2 *Joy:* Jesus' joy is now full. The disciples' joy is mentioned twice: at the beginning, 'disbelieving for joy' (v 41), joy that is too good to be true, that they cannot let themselves believe in; then at the end, unbounded joy – 'they ... returned to Jerusalem with great joy ... blessing God' (vv 52-53). This is the joy reflected in the Lucan canticles, *Magnificat* and *Benedictus*, which we saw had become the Christian prayers of thankful praise for the blessings that Jesus brings to us. So we participate in that joy and it becomes the source of our praise of God. Which stage of the disciples' reaction best fits your feelings at this time? Is it still 'disbelieving for joy', a joy restrained and undermined by difficulties about belief, worries about your worthiness or health? It is not too good to be true! It is true! And if it is true, then we must be joyful and praise God. The Lord wishes us all to come to that second stage, heart-felt rejoicing that Jesus has overcome sin and death, and sits at the right hand of the Father, giving us the gifts of the Spirit. The Lord wishes us to share his joy. How do the disciples in this narrative come to the fullness of joy? They recognise Jesus, listen to his words, allow him to change their views about what has happened, and they worship him. All this happens to them in one appearance of the Lord – it may take a little longer with us, a process that requires much listening, reflecting, praying. That has been the purpose of our working through these sections of the gospel of Luke, like Theophilus, to have a better grasp of what we believe and make it part of ourselves. May we come to say with Mary, 'My soul magnifies the Lord, and my spirit rejoices in God my Saviour' (1:46-7).

3.3 Personal: Jesus in glory does not forget his disciples. He still wishes to be in the midst of them, he brings them peace (v 36). *Shalom*, peace, is a very important concept in Luke. It means in the Bible a sharing in the wholeness of God himself. Appropriately at the beginning of the adventure of salvation, it comes from heaven in the message of the angel at the birth of Jesus: 'Peace on earth among those whom [God] favours' (2:14), and at the end of the gospel it is brought by Jesus himself from the throne of the Father, 'Peace be with you' (v 36). But the disciples are still fragmented by all that has happened, faith mixed with doubt, joy with fear (vv 38, 41). Jesus with great patience calms their fears, helps them to recognise that he is the same person they knew before Calvary, though not just the same. He shows them his hands and feet, invited them to touch him (in both Luke and John we are not told that the disciples in fact touched him; perhaps they somehow did not need to). He talks to them and eats with them. Fear begins to give way to awe, and at the end to worship. The relationship reaches a new level. It is not so familiar, no one makes hasty statements, no one speaks except Jesus in the whole passage. They sense the change, the glory of the new relationship, more demanding, potentially more joy-filled. He leads them through the scriptures, helps them to overcome the 'scandal of the cross', the total stumbling block of his ignominious death. 'Thus it is written that the Messiah is to suffer, and to rise from the dead on the third day' (v 46): so it is part of God's plan, foretold, and leading to glory. With dawning understanding they listen to him asking them to be his witnesses, to proclaim the message of 'repentance and forgiveness of sins' (v 47) to all nations. Jesus knows they cannot do this on their own, and assures them that the Father's promise will be fulfilled: 'Stay here in the city until you have been clothed with power from on high' (v 49). Then he blesses them like Aaron the High Priest of old, and ascends to heaven in their sight. They are filled with joy and worship him (v 52), and praise God in the temple. Their relationship with Jesus, so cruelly tested by the crucifixion, is now restored, and fills them with joy. Henceforth they will find him in their midst in his word, in the breaking of bread, and in the power of the Spirit. Interestingly, in Luke, both here and in Acts, there is never any mention of the disciples being gathered together in fear; they go openly to the temple praising God. In Acts they gather in the upper room, but in prayer, obedient to Jesus' instruction to remain in the city until the coming of the Spirit. Though it is a cliché to say they were hiding in fear, it is only in John 20:19 that 'the doors of the house where the disciples had met were locked for fear of the Jews'. Typically, Luke has no mention of this fear among the disciples; they wait obediently in prayer until the Holy Spirit comes.

How does our own relationship with Jesus fit into all this? Unlike them we have not seen him before or after the resurrection. We may have residual fears, we may not quite believe that Jesus brings peace to our hearts. Learn from the passage how Jesus wants to overcome the doubts of all disciples, wants to be with us, wants to teach us through his word. Suffering is still a stumbling block to many people, our own or that of our loved ones, or the shameful suffering of the poor and the hungry in the world. Those who are in that situation need peace and healing from the risen Lord. Imagine you are a disciple in that room when the Lord appears. Let yourself share the doubts and fears of the disciples, watch Jesus attempting to allay your fears and doubts. Listen as he explains how suffering can be a path to glory. He wants to choose you, me, as a witness to him, to give us the power of the Holy Spirit to enable us to speak out our faith in him. Allow his powerful presence to bring us from fear to awe to worship. Nothing other than a close relationship with the Risen Jesus will be enough to fit us for the mission.

3.4 Challenge: 'You are witnesses to these things' (v 48). There it is, the challenge! The disciples are to be without the physical sight of him, to believe that he is with them, to go and make his

message of repentance and forgiveness known to all nations –
just like that! A scary mission. They are of course not to attempt
it on their own. And 'all nations' begins always with the one you
are in, the people around you, mission territory all of it now
(again). We know that after Pentecost the disciples were fired
with enthusiasm to spread the word, fearless of opposition, glad
to suffer for the sake of his name. The challenge to us is to be witnesses by what we say and do, again not on our own, but with
the strength of the Holy Spirit. We are challenged to be Mary
and Martha of Bethany: to be prayerful like Mary, and pray for
the spread of the gospel; to be active like her sister Martha, and
do things, be active in our parishes, our communities, support
our missionaries, work for the poor. Perhaps also the challenge
is to the Mary in us to be active as well as prayerful, and to the
Martha in us to be more prayerful as well as being active. How
do you feel about this challenge? In what ways can you be a witness in your family, your parish, in the wider community? What
obstacles seem to stand in your way? How could you get round
them?

4. RESPONSE

The disciples at the end of the gospel respond with worship and
joyful praise. 'And they worshipped him, and returned to
Jerusalem with great joy; and they were continually in the temple
blessing God.' (vv 52-3) Follow their lead. Spend some time
worshipping Jesus, the Risen Lord, now seated at the right hand
of God our Father; but also still here in the midst of us, in the
community of those who believe, among us through his word,
his Eucharistic presence and in the power of the Spirit. Give
glory to the Father, Son and Holy Spirit for the great mystery of
salvation through the death and resurrection of Jesus and the
outpouring of the Spirit. Bless the Lord, my soul, and let all that
is within me bless his holy name.

Response in words is not enough. I must respond in action.
Pray for the grace to renew our determination to keep nourish-
ing our minds and hearts with the word of God, to listen to Jesus
as he interprets scripture for us, gives us the Spirit to understand
and put it into practice. Pray for a renewal of our faith in the
Eucharist, in the communal gathering where the word is pro-

claimed, where we are called to repentance and seek forgiveness of sins, where the bread of the Eucharist is broken in the church's living remembrance of the Paschal Mystery, where we are nourished by the Bread of Life. And pray that we may be doers of the word, not just hearers, and people who live the Eucharist, not just pray it. Lord, help us to allow our worship to so strengthen us that we may live our faith in the world around us, and be true witnesses in word and deed.

5. CONTEMPLATION

Our privilege and joy is to live in awareness of the Risen Jesus in us and among us, and the power of the Holy Spirit enlightening our minds, strengthening our will, and stiffening our back-bones. We are able to bless the Lord quietly as we follow our daily routines. Choose a text to keep in our minds and hearts: e.g. 'Jesus said to them, Peace be with you'; or 'You are witnesses to these things', or 'Forgiveness of sins is to be proclaimed in his name to all nations'; or 'They were continually in the temple blessing God.'

Prayer:

As Luke has done in the gospel, we will end where we began, with a Canticle of praise to God, thanking him for the blessing of salvation. We began with the *Magnificat*, we end with the *Benedictus* (1:68-79 NRSV version). These Canticles became and have remained the prayers of praise of the Christian community for the salvation wrought for us in Christ. Notice how the Canticle of Zechariah puts the message that is to be proclaimed by the disciples to all nations into the mission of John the Baptist: 'You will go before the Lord to prepare his ways, to give knowledge of salvation to his people by the forgiveness of their sins.'

Blessed be the Lord God of Israel,
for he has looked favourably on his people and redeemed them.
He has raised up a mighty saviour for us
in the house of his servant David,
as he spoke through the mouth of his holy prophets from of old,

that we would be saved from our enemies
and from the hand of all who hate us.
Thus he has shown the mercy promised to our ancestors,
and has remembered his holy covenant,
the oath that he swore to our ancestor Abraham,
to grant us that we, being rescued from the hands of our
enemies,
might serve him without fear,
in holiness and righteousness before him all our days.
And you, child, will be called the prophet of the Most High,
for you will go before the Lord to prepare his ways,
to give knowledge of salvation to his people
by the forgiveness of their sins.
By the tender mercy of our God,
the dawn from on high will break upon us,
to give light to those who sit in darkness and in the shadow
of death,
to guide our feet into the way of peace.